VIOLENT OBSESSION

THE STALKER NEXT DOOR

The amazing true story of
lust, fixation, courage and survival

Jackie Eigner
and
Simon Gullifer

First published in 2016 by Barrallier Books Pty Ltd,
trading as Echo Books

Registered Office: 35-37 Gordon Avenue, West Geelong, Victoria 3220,
Australia.

www.echobooks.com.au

National Library of Australia Cataloguing-in-Publication entry.

Creator: Eigner, Jackie, author.

Title: Violent obsession : the stalker next door : the amazing true story of
lust, fixation, courage and survival/Jackie Eigner, Simon Gullifer.

ISBN: 9780994491121 (paperback)

Subjects: Eigner, Joan. Stalking victims--United States. Stalkers--United
States. Stalking--United States. Women--Crimes against--United States.

Dewey Number: 364.1580973

Book and cover design by Peter Gamble, Canberra.

Set in Garamond Premier Pro Display, 12/17 and Minerva, Small Caps/
Modern.

www.echobooks.com.au

For Joan–a wonderfully selfless and resilient woman.

Particularly to those who know her well, this story will not seem real. The eternal optimist, she never speaks of her suffering. But we know the fear she masks and the damage she buries. Since embarking on this book, many have challenged her intention to publish her story, asking whether it will only serve to ignite her stalker's hatred. Her answer is always the same: 'It doesn't matter.'

There is a dignity in her resignation and her strength is moving. She knows that the man who has caused her so many years of abject fear is never going to leave her alone. And we champion her refusal to be a silent victim any longer. Sharing her experience was far from easy for her; and for many of those who know her, they will be learning of her true pain for the first time.

This is her story.

CONTENTS

Foreword — vii
Prologue — xi
Timeline of events — xvii
Part one: Cast of characters
    Cast of characters — 3
    The Stalked — 5
    Lester Lyle Worthington — 15
Part two: Living with Lester
    How it all began — 23
    Is anybody listening? — 27
    Joan's nightmare — 31
    The final straw — 45
    Taking action — 51
    Stroke of genius — 55
    Hung jury — 61
    A confusing conviction — 79
    He's back — 83
    Another trial — 91
    Lester targets the LMSV School District — 97
    Justice at long last — 105
    Bittersweet — 125
    One more battle — 131
    Joan reflects — 141

Part three: Stalking resources
    What is stalking?   145
    The history of stalking   153
    Why stalkers stalk   163
    Assisting victims   169
A note on sources   175

FOREWORD

If this story were not true, it would be unbelievable. There are just so many elements that defy belief: a man who would never give up on his fantasies, a woman who survived years of abuse but was taken to the edge of sanity; and a justice system that was ill-equipped to assist a helpless victim.

This is the story of Joan Eigner, a devoted wife and loving mother, and her struggle to survive twenty-four years of torment at the hands of Lester Lyle Worthington, a cruel and remorseless stalker. Despite numerous court appearances and several stints in prison, Lester's thirst for Joan would never wane. In 2011, twenty-four years after his obsession began, he would receive his longest prison sentence yet—just over eight years—for his unrelenting abuse of her and her family. As dictated by California law, Lester was eligible for parole after serving only half of his sentence. So in February 2015, Joan and her family prepared for the likelihood that they would have to relive the nightmare all over again.

But in a bizarre twist of fate only too common to this story, Lester would be deemed mentally disordered only days before his scheduled release and transferred to the Atascadero State Hospital—a secure psychiatric hospital in Central California. He remains incarcerated at Atascadero at the time of writing this book and is unlikely to be assessed for release until 2019.

The Eigners were an ordinary, middleclass suburban family from Southern California. Joan and Akira were vibrant, active and loving parents consumed by the demands of raising their three young children and indulging an exhaustive list of extracurricular activities. There was nothing in particular that set them apart from the average family. There was nothing that Joan did that could justify why she would become the center of this nightmare. Besides a natural beauty and humble grace, there was certainly nothing that could explain why she became the target of Lester's lust, fixation and anger.

Joan and Lester were never lovers. They were never friends. They have never even had a conversation. They were simply neighbors. He would first see her in 1979 when his family moved into the house next door to hers. She was twenty-one and beautiful and he was just a teenager. For many years he was just the kid next door. Joan never thought he was a threat. In fact, she didn't think much of him at all.

But this would all change on March 1, 1988 when she would catch him trying to break into her bedroom. The Sheriff's Department was called and his fingerprints were found on the door. But he was never charged. It seemed he had gotten away with a crime and knew it. With a bolstered confidence, his obsessions with her were born. But in 1988, stalking had yet to be criminalized.

For the next five years, Lester blazed a tyrannical trail of abuse against Joan and her family including attempted assaults, verbal abuse, threats to kill, prank phone calls, lewd gestures and constantly following her. She would eventually be forced to live like a prisoner: locking doors when she was home, staying inside if he was out, altering her routines to avoid him and repeatedly changing her telephone number. In fact, his stalking of Joan would become common knowledge in the neighborhood. But they were powerless to help her.

Time and time again Joan pleaded with the local Sheriff's Department for assistance. But time and time again she was denied it. Years later, one of the Deputy Sheriffs admitted to her that they had even begun to call her 'that crazy lady'. For Joan, it felt like they either didn't care or had no idea how to deal with Lester's harassment—even after stalking was criminalized in 1990. But finally, five years after Lester's abuse started, one Detective took pity on her and investigated her claims properly. What happened next shocked him.

To this day, the rationale for Lester's next brazen move remains a mystery. Inexplicably, Lester turned his attentions to the Detective and began stalking both him and his family. He followed the Detective, threatened the Detective's wife and children, and made wild allegations that Joan and the Detective were romantically involved. For going after one of their own, Lester had now gained the attention of the local Sheriff's Department. This was a frustrating but ultimately welcome irony for Joan. She was no longer the 'crazy lady'. She was finally recognized as a victim.

In 1994, Lester pleaded guilty to stalking Joan. He was sent to prison and Joan believed the ordeal was over. It would take time, but eventually she returned to a somewhat normal life. She could leave the house and do the things that mothers do and walk the streets without looking over her shoulder. But four years later, a phone call would change all of that. It was from Lester's parole officer. The officer warned her that Lester wanted revenge and that he had tried to buy a gun. Joan thanked the officer and hung up the phone. She didn't know how to respond. Having moved to a new house by that stage, she just hoped Lester wouldn't find her and tried to go on living her life the best she could.

For the next nine years, it seemed that she could. But, as he always did, Lester found her. In a calculated and cunning feat, he managed to get a job where Joan worked. Despite being fired within days of starting his new job, the damage had been done. He had found Joan and there was no way he was letting her go. He pursued her with a venom and ferocity that he had never exhibited before. He tried to hire someone to set fire to her home, he tried to hire someone to hurt her, and a vehicle at her work was firebombed. In 2011, he would finally be stopped when he was arrested, tried and sentenced to prison.

To this day, Joan has no idea why he picked her. If you ask him, he will tell you that they had been lovers. He would tell you that they had embarked on a passionate affair that she abruptly ended. He would tell you that she was his 'first love' and that she taught him how to 'make love'. It would probably all sound fairly plausible, but it is simply not true.

PROLOGUE

There are very few moments in life that we remember with utter clarity. You know the type: a moment where all of the senses are recalled without the slightest effort. When we describe these memories, we often say things like 'hair-raising', or 'took my breath away'. For me, these moments have included the birth of my children, helping my daughters deliver their babies and the moment I watched my father take his last breath. But there are also those that I truly wish I could forget. These are the scars that Lester Worthington has carved into my life.

I often reflect on the person that I was when all this started. I was a young mother with three children. I always knew that I wanted to be a mom and my children were everything to me. They still are. My world was uncomplicated and involved the usual things: family, friends, church and work. I had no idea of what was to come and had no reason to think that this would ever happen to me. I was trusting, probably even naïve. I knew what a stalker was, but had no idea what it actually meant. I certainly had no idea about police investigations, the criminal justice system, or the wrenching experience of giving evidence in court.

All this changed though when Lester came into our lives. I was slow to realize that he was more than just an obsessively curious and odd neighbor.

There was a wickedness about him that is hard to put into words. In time, it became all too clear that he wanted to poison every part of my life. I had no idea why he did the things that he did. I kept hoping that he would realize what he was doing was wrong and that he would stop. But he never did.

As the months turned into years, the taunts and threats became more perverse and brazen. I became more and more nervous and anxious. There was always a dark cloud hanging over my head. I had three children and wanted their lives to be normal. But the stress and anxiety were crushing as I fought to shield them from the maniac next door. Like most mothers, I wanted my kids to have a healthy and happy upbringing. I know now that in trying to achieve this, my own mental and physical health suffered significantly.

I have always been private about my emotions, but especially with this experience. I found it incredibly embarrassing to speak about Lester and the things he did to me. I very rarely spoke about him or the overwhelming impact it was having on my life. I had a few people in whom I confided, but looking back now, they had no idea how to advise me. They had never been in any circumstance remotely similar and often remarked that they have never heard of anything so incredible.

I wanted my children to see me as being strong and protective. In the times when it became too much for me to handle, I didn't want them to see their mom falling apart. I would often leave the house to cry. No child should have to see that. Sometimes I would find myself in the dugout of a nearby softball field. I would sit there alone and sob in desperation. Other times I would sit in my car and just break down. I am still private about my whole experience. Up until now, I have shared my story with only a few people in my life.

I would try to hide the things that Lester did to me. It even came to a point when I didn't want to tell my own husband. I felt it wasn't worth the emotional drain from his response. At times he would become angry and leave me feeling like there was something I could and should be doing to make Lester stop. Sometimes he made me feel like it was my fault. Maybe that was just his way of showing support, but it didn't feel supportive. I am not sure if he ever truly understood what I was going through.

Psychologically, I was always on edge. It was excruciating. I lived in a state of constant fear and was always trying to make sense out of this crazy situation. I was always wondering how I could make it stop. I spent most of my time looking over my shoulder and simply waiting for the next episode of abuse. I was scared that the next time he would physically hurt me or one of my kids. No one should have to live like that. It is just not fair to feel that afraid.

I desperately wanted my life to get back to normal, but I had no idea how to get it there. It was crippling. I became a prisoner in my own home. I didn't want to go out. I didn't want to give Lester any reason to see me. I became a complete social recluse and didn't want to put my children in harm's way. It is a horrible feeling knowing that there is someone constantly there—someone watching your every move. And it is even worse to question your ability to keep your own children safe.

My emotional suffering through all of this was immeasurable. Even now, I can't describe it. I remember at one stage telling my sister that I felt like humpty-dumpty—like I had been shattered into a thousand pieces and would never be put back together again. Besides the fear and the constant torment of Lester's antics, I had to go through one tortuous process after another. There were police statements to give, pre-trials and trials to testify at, and numerous restraining orders that I had to apply for and defend. In total, I would be made to sit in the witness stand seven times to rid this man from my life.

After years of being ignored by police, I was always afraid the Judge or jury would dismiss my claims as just the rants of a crazy woman. After all, that is what the local Sheriff's Department had apparently dubbed me by the time anyone finally took my complaints seriously.

When you are forced to sit in front of an entire courtroom, including the man who has wronged you, and convince them all that you are not lying, you are stripped completely bare. You have no protections against the personal insults and mockery that are just cornerstones of an adversarial justice system. Nothing could really prepare you for that experience.

When the first restraining order against Lester was granted, I was sitting in the courtroom and I just broke down. An overwhelming amount of emotion—fear, apprehension, hate, disgust, relief—just came pouring out. I remember thinking that things were finally going to stop, that life would finally get back to normal. But the very next day, Lester violated the order. I called the Sheriff's Department, but they refused to come out. Clear as anything, I remember hanging up the phone and for the first time in my life, I had suicidal thoughts. I told myself, 'Just go pick up the gun and shoot yourself. This whole thing will be over. You will never have to deal with it again.'

After what I perceived to be repeated failures of the justice system, I began to feel like this was just something I would have to live with and deal with on my own. And in a way, it was. Emotionally, I have buried so much of the deep frustration and desperation I felt at that time. I keep it locked away in a place where I don't have to live and I have learned not to let those memories define who I am.

I know that Lester may one day be a free man. I know that my current sense of security is measured. While this is easy to write, the reality of it is much more difficult. Anyone who is in a similar situation would agree. At the moment, while he is locked away, I am less consumed by thoughts of the future. But I know the day may come when I will have to start asking myself the hard questions: Will I leave my home? If so, where will I go? Could I leave my children and grandchildren for a new city? But I try to take each day as it comes. If I dwell on these things, I quickly become overwhelmed. I don't want to give Lester satisfaction.

I know this experience has forever scarred me. I know that in many ways it has shaped who I am today—for better or worse. I sometimes think about the last twenty-eight years—all the fear, helplessness and torment; the struggle to be taken seriously or fake my appearance of normality when I am feeling anything but normal—and I wonder who I would have been if this had not happened to me. I know I have a strong independent way about me now and I have no doubt some see me as uncompromising. But I would rather do things myself than ask for help. Perhaps this stems from years of feeling let down when I needed help the most.

I also know that I can be hyper-vigilant and unnecessarily nervous. For example, when a strange man approaches me, even if only to ask an innocent question, my first reaction is fear. Or if a car paces next to mine while I am driving, I am hit with an inexplicable wave of anxiety and have to immediately slow down. If my phone rings and the caller does not respond after I say 'hello,' I can not hang up quickly enough. I have a very hard time trusting people and it takes me a long time to grow close to others. I am also painfully private about my life.

By far the most common thing people ask me is 'why'? 'Why did he choose you'? Funnily enough, that is the most common thing I have asked myself for twenty-eight years. I know it sounds unbelievable and it probably isn't the answer most people want to hear, but the truth is: I don't know. I really do not know. And for so many years I have tormented and searched myself for an answer. For a while, I even convinced myself that I must have done something because—I thought—people don't just start stalking someone for no reason. I would play it back over and over in my head until I allowed myself to believe that I must have given him the wrong signal. I started to think that maybe it was my fault.

How naïve I was. And how many thousands of victims must torture themselves in the same manner—trying to find reason in someone else's insanity. It is human nature. Humans want to believe there is a reason why things happen, we want to have someone or something to blame. If this has taught me anything at all, it would be that sometimes things happen for no reason, and there are few things in life over which we have total control.

I am sick of hiding. I am sick of running from this man that has caused me so many years of unjust pain and terror. I am tired of reading about victims who are forced to change their lives to survive their tormentors. In fact, just tonight as I write this, the news is headlining a story about a distraught ex-lover who walked into his ex-girlfriend's work and opened fire. When all was said and done, not only was she dead, but four of her coworkers as well. The victim had a restraining order against the shooter, but that proved useless in protecting her. I am sick of hearing these stories. Only now do I understand that I am meant to tell mine.

In 2011, after Lester's last criminal trial, I asked my daughter to write this book. A criminologist by profession, she questioned my decision to publish my story. Indeed many people have including members of the Sheriff's Department and the District Attorney's office. But for me, my voice is all I have. Come what may, I can no longer accept that victims are expected to hide in silence. We are expected to bury our fear and sense of injustice as we hope our lives will one day return to normal. As much as Lester scares me, he infuriates me. How dare he think he can rob me of my basic freedoms and my peace of mind. In telling my story, I want to advocate for every other victim of this selfish crime. You are not alone.

Everything in this book is true. I have recounted my stories exactly as I remember them. Some names have been changed to protect those individuals and I have asked the authors to withhold certain aspects of my private life, both past and present. There are some things that I never want to share with Lester; he has taken enough of me already.

Joan Eigner

Timeline of events

1979   Eigners move into 9809 Via Francis, Santee, California

        Worthingtons move into home next door to Eigners

1988   Lester begins stalking Joan

1990   Stalking is criminalized in the state of California

1993   Joan files a civil complaint (*Eigner v Worthington*)

        San Diego Superior Court issue a restraining order against Lester

        First criminal trial is held (*People v Lester Lyle Worthington*)

1994   Lester pleads guilty to Stalking and Violating a Court Order

1995   Joan and Akira Eigner divorce

1998   Lester's probation officer warns Joan

2007   Lester obtains a job at Joan's work

2008   San Diego Superior Court issue a restraining order against Lester

2009   Lester solicits someone to hurt Joan

        Second criminal trial is held (*People v Lester Lyle Worthington*)

        Lester begins stalking another victim

2010   Lester targets Joan again

2011   Third criminal trial is held (*People v Lester Lyle Worthington*)

        Lester is convicted and sentenced to eight years in prison

2015   Lester is transferred to Atascadero State Hospital—a secure
                psychiatric facility

PART ONE: CAST OF CHARACTERS

CAST OF CHARACTERS

Joan Eigner: Stalked by Lester Lyle Worthington since 1988.
Akira Eigner: Joan's husband to 1995.
Joe Eigner: Eldest son of Joan and Akira.
Jackie Eigner: Eldest daughter of Joan and Akira.
Juliann Eigner: Youngest daughter of Joan and Akira.
Mark: Joan's husband since 2000.
Lester Lyle Worthington: Has stalked Joan Eigner since 1988.
Gloria Worthington: Mother of Lester.
Darren*: Stalked by Lester in 2009.
Detective Howard Bradley: Lead investigator, 1993 to 1995.
Attorney Charles 'Chuck' Nachand: Initiated civil proceedings, 1993.
Detective Wood*: Lead investigator, 2009 and 2011.
Attorney Marian Birge: Advocate for Joan, 2015.

---

* Not his real name

THE STALKED

Joan Marie Bennett was born in 1957 in a small Southern Californian town called La Habra. Roughly twenty miles from Los Angeles, La Habra was little more than a rural working-class suburb at the time. For her father, an ordained pastor and retired serviceman, it was a good place to raise a large family on a modest wage.

Joan was the fifth of six girls born to her parents, James ('Jim') and Virginia ('Jean') Bennett. Jim was a deeply religious man and a strict disciplinarian and Jean was a devoted mother. Having met and dated in their hometown in Kentucky, Jim proposed to Jean shortly before he left for his naval deployment to San Diego, California. Jean was only seventeen at the time, but she said 'yes' and joined him as soon as she turned eighteen.

Several years later, Jean gave birth to their first daughter. Eventually they would have five more. Each of those six daughters would go on to marry and have families of their own and by the time they had both passed away, they would boast a lineage of six daughters, twenty-two grandchildren and thirty-six great grandchildren.

When Joan was born, her parents were already struggling to fit their gaggle of girls into their small family home. Despite adding an extra bedroom, the five girls still had to squeeze into two bedrooms. When her last sister was born, the girls slept three to each room. Despite the obvious propensity for territorial and hormonal fights, Joan remembers her childhood with fondness. Her father adored horses and made sure the girls all grew up riding. The beauty of a very small house on a very large block meant there was always room for various pets. Among the girls, there was also always a willing playmate on hand and loneliness was simply not possible. As the Bennett girls got older, their home was naturally a magnet for adolescent boys.

Joan was a reserved and compliant child and navigated her schooling with ease. She was painfully shy, but pursued her love of singing as a member of her school and church choirs and swam for the school squad. She completed her high school studies within three years and graduated. She was desperate for independence and adventure, so, promising her parents it was only temporary, she left for Maui to live with one of her older sisters.

It was eight months of pure bliss. She quickly found a housekeeping job at a resort located in a remote area of the island. She worked at night and spent the rest of her days on Maui's unspoiled beaches. The serene and peaceful pace of the island suited her well and she fell in love with her new life. Then her mother started calling.

Jean was desperately anxious for Joan to return home. She had already lost four daughters to marriage and jobs that moved them away from home and she couldn't stomach Joan being so far from her. Joan was about to apply to the local community college to study nursing, but Jean wouldn't waiver. Joan didn't know how to disobey her mother, but she managed to reach a compromise they could both live with. So with a sense of sadness and excitement, she said goodbye to her sister and beloved Maui and headed for the funky streets of Pacific Beach in San Diego.

Better known as 'PB', Pacific Beach was an eclectic seaside town just north of downtown San Diego. Best known for its surfing and nightlife, it was a great place to be young and carefree. Joan had two older sisters living in PB at the time and they agreed to keep an eye on her. So her mother assented to the arrangement, unaware that within months, Joan would meet Akira, a Japanese-born hippie eight years her senior, and that they would marry a short time later.

Akira was rebellious, wild and the life of any party. He had a love for music, fast cars, bell-bottom pants and a long ponytail. Having very little in common in their pasts, their interests and their way of life, they couldn't have been any more different. Her sisters tried to keep them apart, telling Joan she was far too young to settle down. They even hid Joan's car once to keep her from seeing him. But despite their efforts, the pair quickly fell in love, and Joan soon became pregnant. In a whirl of happiness and romance, they eloped to a quaint church in the nearby country town of Julian.

The following March, Joan gave birth to their first child. They named him Joseph, but everyone called him Joey. Once he was a teenager, he would drop the 'y' and has gone by 'Joe' ever since. At the time of his birth, the couple was renting a small one-bedroom apartment in Pacific Beach and Akira was working as a truck loader (and later as a delivery driver) for the United Parcel Service (UPS). Akira prided himself in his work and was often away from home for long hours, but he loved providing for his little family.

Joan was delighted to be a stay-at-home mom. Joe was a beautifully spirited baby, but he was a terrible sleeper. She would spend hours rocking him through the night but the thin apartment walls did little to contain his unrelenting crying. To fend off complaints from the neighbors, they would often get into the car in the middle of the night and drive aimlessly while their baby slept. But after several months of this midnight routine, they knew it was time to move.

The couple moved inland to the eastern suburbs of San Diego to a much larger townhouse in Poway. Now known as the 'city in the country', Poway was a quiet town sandwiched between bolder-blazoned mountains. Akira didn't mind the longer commute and Joan wiled away her days with a busy toddler. Shortly after Joe turned two, Joan gave birth to their second child.

Throughout the pregnancy, Joan prayed for a girl to round out her growing family. When the doctor confirmed it moments after Jackie was born, she remembers shouting, 'Well praise the Lord!' She felt truly blessed for the birth of baby Jacquelynn, who would always go by 'Jackie'.

Soon after Jackie was born, Joan and Akira decided they wanted a bigger house with a yard for their rambunctious kids to play in and they began hunting for a new home. They set their sights on a new housing development in the budding town of Santee.

Santee was another eastern suburb of San Diego, not far from Poway and about eighteen miles from the coast. Now a populous suburban community, in 1978 Santee was little more than a rural town nestled at the base of rolling hills and Cowles Mountain, the highest point in San Diego. The scenic beauty and small town feel of Santee appealed to both Joan and Akira, so when they found an elevated block of land in a quiet cul-de-sac, with a big backyard and views to the eastern mountains, they thought their dreams had come true. They fought hard to secure that block of land, an irony that is not lost on either of them because soon after they moved in, Lester and his family arrived next door.

For the next few years, Akira kept busy with work and Joan relished in her role as a fulltime housewife and mother. She enrolled Joe in a mommy-and-me preschool that met one day per week and helped with the class program. When Jackie was two she started hanging wallpaper for her sister's business one day a week. It was just enough time away from the house and two busy kids to balance the chaos of full-time motherhood.

Life was rather uneventful, but it was good. By now, the Worthington family had moved in next door. Gloria Worthington was a widow and a single mom of five adult kids. They were a rowdy bunch, but it was Gloria's youngest, Lester, who quickly earned a reputation as the neighborhood nuisance. He was often racing his car up and down the street and admitted using a range of illicit drugs on a regular basis.

The Worthington home was a large two-story house that was almost perfectly rectangular in shape. One of its best features was a sprawling timber balcony that wrapped around the entire upper level of the back of the house. Like the Eigners' home, it sat atop a small hill that overlooked the busy street intersection below. The balcony served as a perfect viewing deck into the Eigners' backyard and a stage upon which Lester would often poise.

Up until this time, Joan had lived a fairly quiet and sheltered life and had never been exposed to behavior quite like Lester's. While his affections and actions were not yet aimed at her or her children, she was still apprehensive of him and his family. Gloria was a quiet woman who kept to herself. In the early days, Joan tried to exchange pleasantries with her when their paths crossed, but her greetings were always met with a stony silence. She never knew whether it was disinterest or disdain that kept Gloria from engaging with her, but after a few failed attempts to be neighborly, Joan stopped trying.

By the time Joe and Jackie were old enough to run around in the front yard together, there was an apparent understanding and acceptance between the two women that they weren't going to be friends. Joan never held any ill will towards Gloria, but she would never feel comfortable in her presence.

In 1982, Joan became pregnant with their last child. Although the pregnancy was a complete surprise, the entire family was ecstatic to meet the final member of their family. In April the following year, she gave birth to Juliann. From the start, Juliann was a vivacious and bubbly baby and everyone enjoyed her beyond words. The two older kids fought over who would push her stroller, feed her, bathe her and everything in between. They called her the happy Buddha baby because of her unfathomable rolls of baby fat and permanent drool-drenched smile. She was a delightful baby, and Joan truly felt that her world was complete.

Life became hectic. Joan juggled her newborn baby with taxiing her older kids to endless sporting practices, games and play-dates. At only one week old, Julliann became the youngest spectator in the bleachers of Joe's baseball games. At night, there was homework and the usual long list of domestic chores. And with two growing children, there was never a moment's peace. But Joan preferred it that way. She loved having a house full of kids, but mostly she loved having her kids where she could keep an eye on them.

While the real terrifying behavior was yet to come, Joan always worried for her children's safety when Lester was around and she would do her best to shield her kids from his erratic behaviors. At times this was difficult given that they lived next door, but also because Lester would engage in games with the neighborhood kids. Despite being much older, he would join them in a game of baseball or football in the street.

Then one day, Joan's fears were confirmed when Jackie told her that Lester had asked her into his home. She would have been as young as six. In a statement to the San Diego District Attorney, Jackie remembered:

> It was during these early years and interactions that [he] invited me into his home for 'milk and cookies' and to look at his bedroom. This happened on at least three occasions that I can recall. I remember standing on his doorstep and peering into his home while he made these invitations, but I never did enter into his home. I recall him telling me he had some photos in his bedroom that he wanted to show me.

> I asked what they were and he told me the photos were of
> me and my family. I remember feeling odd and scared at
> the time that he would have such photos. I remember I told
> my mother about his proposition and the photos and she
> reiterated that we were to stay away from [him].

Akira was very lucky to have the amount of vacation leave that UPS afforded him and he took the family on regular holidays. There were annual road-trips to visit his family in Washington State and as the kids got older ski trips to Southern California's mountain resorts. Always a fan of open roads and long drives, he piled the family into the car every summer and they would head to America's beautiful Northwest. Along the way, there were stops in any number of the amazing national parks on offer throughout California, Nevada and Oregon and they would camp, bike, hike and fish. It was fantastic fun. Joan and Akira were vibrant and young parents and they showered their children in travel and outdoor activities: no doubt breeding in them a love of adventure that they would all later engender in adulthood.

By the time that Juliann turned three, Joan felt ready to take on a permanent part-time job. So when a family friend asked if she would be interested in cleaning pools for his small company, she was excited. For her, it was the perfect job. Not only would she be working outside in the Southern Californian sun, she could organize her cleanings around her kids' busy school and sporting schedules. While she only made a small wage, it was extra spending money for the family and allowed her the odd occasion to spoil herself (something every mother deserves). But she would eventually be forced to quit this job when Lester began following her and appearing at her scheduled cleanings.

In 1990, she started working as a school bus driver for the La Mesa Spring Valley (LMSV) School District, a job that she would keep until her retirement in early 2015. While her own kids were young, she thought it was the perfect job. She mostly worked during school hours and had all of the same vacation days as her kids. But all too soon this job would also prove fraught with danger when Lester again began to follow and threaten her while she drove students on her bus.

As Lester's harassment intensified, she fought to lead a normal life, but Joan knew she had been forever changed. Once an ordinary and happy family, there was no way of foretelling the destruction that Lester would wreak on her, her family, and everything they had worked towards. After many years of frustration, sadness and growing resentment, Joan and Akira's relationship finally fractured and they agreed to divorce in 1995 after nineteen years of marriage.

For the first time in her adult life, Joan was single. It was frightening, but it was also liberating. She kept busy with work and insulated herself in the protection of strong friendships and church. The family home on Via Francis Street was sold and she and the kids moved to a rental house across town. While she dabbled in dating, she couldn't muster the energy to pursue a fulltime relationship. Instead, she focused on recovering from a difficult divorce and trying to claw her way out of an ever-increasing debt from raising three kids on a bus driver's wage. Fortunately, it was also during these healing years that Lester's obsession went dormant. He had just finished serving his first prison stint for stalking her and he wouldn't emerge again for nine years.

When she least expected it, Joan fell in love with a man named Mark. He had three sons, all close in age to her kids, and was a fellow enthusiast of the outdoors. After six months of hiking and dinner dates, the topic of marriage was discussed. Joan was truly taken by Mark, but she surprised even herself when she said yes to his proposal. They wed in 2000 and remain happily married. They are still avid adventurists and are doting grandparents to thirteen children.

AKIRA

Akira was born in Kumamoto, Japan in 1949. At the age of five, his mother, Kiyoko, divorced his abusive father and left Akira and his younger brother, Kenji, in her mother's care. Several years later, Kiyoko met and married Robert Eigner, an American naval officer serving in Sasebo, Japan. Robert adopted Akira and Kenji and he and Kiyoko had two more sons of their own. In 1965, Robert brought a heavily pregnant Kiyoko and his four sons to Long Beach, California. It was a three month journey that Akira would never forget. Despite having no understanding of American culture or the English language, Akira graduated from Clairemont High School in San Diego in 1969.

Akira dabbled in university studies, but opted instead to wholly embrace the free spirited climate of the US in the 1970s. In between partying, driving fast cars and attending music festivals, he held various odd jobs. He remembers most fondly his role managing a local car wash. It was during these years that he met Joan. Several months before Joe was born, Akira started working with the UPS.

Akira was an exceptionally hardworking individual. He defined his worth through his ability to provide for his family. In return, he demanded effort and achievement from his children. Despite his long hours at work, he immersed himself in coaching girl's softball—a role he was well known for and would pursue for twenty-five years. In 2005, he retired from the UPS after twenty-six years of service. He remains in San Diego and is thoroughly enjoying retirement.

JOE

Joe was born in March 1976 in San Diego. He graduated from Santana High School in Santee in 1994. As a teenager, he excelled at numerous sports—including tennis and baseball—but found his ultimate passion in surfing and music. Since 2000 he has recorded a number of albums and in 2004, he attained an Associates Degree in cardiovascular technology and has since become a leader in his field. Joe continues to surf and make music most days.

JACKIE

Jackie was born in May 1978 in San Diego. She graduated from Santana High School in 1996. Her childhood was largely consumed by sports and she would earn a full-ride scholarship to San Diego State University for softball. In 2001, she graduated with a Bachelor's Degree in Liberal Arts and Sciences in Sociology. In 2003, she graduated from Bond University in Australia with a Master's Degree in Criminology and has worked in Australian law enforcement ever since.

JULIANN

Juliann was born in April 1983. She graduated from Santana High School in 2001. She was popular, well liked and involved in numerous activities including the student council, drama, and sport. Juliann was a focused and driven young woman and after graduation she worked tireless hours in various jobs to fund her college education. In 2007, she graduated from San Diego State University with a Bachelor's Degree of Science in Nursing. She is currently a head Cardiac Intensive Care Unit nurse and is completing her Master's Degree in Nursing.

LESTER LYLE WORTHINGTON[1]

Lester Lyle Worthington was born on July 21, 1961 in New London, Connecticut. Nicknamed 'the whaling city', New London is a seaport city located on the northeast coast of the US, between Manhattan and Boston. During the nineteenth century, New London made vast revenue from the whaling industry—a wealth that is apparent in the city's charm, historic buildings and idyllic harbor.

When Lester was born, his parents, Robert and Gloria Worthington, already had three sons and one daughter. Lester would be their fifth and last child. When Lester was still in primary school, his family moved to California because of Robert's service with the US Navy. The family settled in San Diego, a natural choice given its large seaports and expansive Naval presence.

It was the late 1960s and the US was well entrenched in the Vietnam War. Robert, a Chief Hospital Corpsman, was soon deployed, leaving behind his large family to serve aboard the swift boats that patrolled the rivers of Vietnam. He would never return home. On April 12, 1969, he was killed when his boat was hit by a Viet Cong rocket in the province of

[1] Information used to produce this chapter was largely sourced from the San Diego Probation Report, 2011.

An Xugen. Lester was only eight years old and Gloria was left to raise five children on her own.

But despite the loss of his father, Lester claims to have had a stable upbringing and a good relationship with his mother. However, he is quick to state that his mother failed to provide sufficient structure and discipline because she was a single parent of five children.

Lester is a loner. He has never been married and has no children. Despite brief stints in prison and rental accommodation, he has lived with his mother for most of his life. He admits to drinking alcohol and smoking marijuana since the age of ten, as well as occasionally using inhalants and hallucinogenic mushrooms as a teenager. According to him, he began using methamphetamine and LSD on a daily basis. He used methamphetamine for approximately five years and LSD for approximately two years. This could account for the erratic behavior that Lester was apparently known for when he first moved to Via Francis Street.

Lester attended Mount Miguel High School in Spring Valley, San Diego. He was a 'D' student in his classes, was frequently truant and described himself as the 'class clown'. He dropped out of high school after his sophomore year, claiming a brain injury held him back from learning. As an adult, he would claim that he suffered three traumatic brain injuries during his lifetime. He believes these injuries have significantly lowered his IQ and have plagued his ability to work. He claims to enjoy activities like skiing, camping, fishing and biking.

Lester claims to suffer from many learning disabilities, including dyslexia and states that he requires repeated guidance to complete tasks or process ideas. He finds verbal instructions extremely difficult to understand, especially if given in complex sentences or ideas. He claims that he functions better when verbal directions are provided in small, easy to process sentences.

When he was eighteen, Lester moved into the house on Via Francis Street with his mother. At any given time, a number of his siblings would also live there, but their arrangement never appeared to be permanent. As an admittedly rebellious and dysfunctional teenager who was often under the influence of drugs, this is when Lester would first see the woman that would fixate him for the rest of his life.

Lester's early dalliances with the law were sporadic. His first contact with the Sheriff's Department for harassing Joan didn't occur until 1988. He was twenty-six years old. Two years later, he was arrested for assaulting his mother and resisting a Deputy Sheriff. According to court records, he came home drunk and demanded money from his mother. When she refused, he pushed her away and punched her in the face. His brother intervened and a separate fight ensued between the two men.

The Sheriff's Department was called and Lester was arrested. He was uncooperative and threatening, telling the arresting officer,

> I could have bashed your face in with my elbow. When I get out I'll meet you with my .357; when I get out in sixteen hours I'll find out where you live ... do you like fires? I'll get even with you, legally or illegally. Do you know who you are dealing with? You're dealing with someone who is crazy. Look into my eyes, I'm crazy!

Lester also spat on the officer and made derogatory sexual remarks to her. He taunted,

> Hey bitch talk to me. What's the matter, don't you like men? Oh, you must be a dyke. You look like a dyke. Is that it? Have you had a seven inch cock? Come on, I'll show you what it feels like. Have you ever had a nine inch cock in your mouth? Come on dyke, talk to me.

Lester has failed to maintain stable employment for most of his adult life. He admits to being fired from at least seven different jobs and has had long stints of unemployment, including the three consecutive years before he was sentenced to jail for stalking Joan in 1994. He claims that his brain injuries are largely responsible for his inability to hold down a job; however, despite these claims, he repeatedly demonstrated a clear understanding of the law, as well as a cunning ability to evade arrest for his continued harassment of Joan. He knew exactly how to navigate the justice system to ensure his own freedom.

On occasion, long periods of time would pass between Lester's contacts with Joan. However, this was more an indication of his sophistication than incidental conduct. He planned his contacts with care. He learned her daily patterns and routines. He memorised her work schedules and pool cleanings and the routes that she drove between them and home. And in approximately late 2006, early 2007, he managed to get a job where she worked. Even her relocation to a new suburb wouldn't stop him from finding her.

Lester was aware of the passage of time between his contacts with Joan. He used this time to justify his claims that he wasn't stalking her. But these periods of time did not serve to reduce the terror for Joan. Instead they reinforced and fed her fear.

By 2011, after multiple convictions for harassing Joan, the San Diego County Probation Department finally concluded that Lester posed a serious risk to society. He had proven to be a poor candidate for probation and the department would recommend that he didn't receive it. He had routinely violated previous probation orders, including failed drug tests, avoiding mandatory reporting requirements, and attempting to buy a gun.

For twenty-eight years, Lester appears to have shown no remorse for his criminal offending. He has never expressed any feelings of empathy for his victims; instead he blames them for his actions. Whether at trial, providing a statement to the Sheriff's Department, or speaking to his probation officer, Lester's position that Joan and her children have pre-empted his ire has never waivered. His obsession with them has never diminished. He can blame a poor family upbringing, previous abuses, brain injuries, mental impairment or the victims themselves; but Joan has never accepted those excuses. She has seen his cunningness. She has seen his glee at getting away with a crime. And she has heard his taunts when he avoided arrest.

In 2011, Lester's probation officer summed up his actions as follows:

> The defendant ... acted with disregard to the safety of the public in his zeal to terrorize his victims. The defendant inflicted emotional injury. The victims are afraid for their safety and the safety of their families ... The manner in which the crime was carried out demonstrated criminal sophistication ...   The defendant sought out his victims at their place of employment to follow them or to make contact with them. He hid in bushes, dressed in camouflage, and searched through employee directories to find Joan W ... He also has other convictions indicating a pattern of violent and unpredictable behavior ... Most disturbing of all, the defendant does not seem to view any of his actions or attitudes as inappropriate, even when these ideas are challenged with more logical and socially acceptable ideas. He seems to have a deeply ingrained pattern of criminal thinking, blaming others for his actions and accepting no personal responsibility ... Without a significant period of custody, it seems likely the defendant is on a collision course with these victims where someone may lose a life.

PART TWO: LIVING WITH LESTER

One cannot imagine fearing for one's life on a daily basis and never knowing which day will bring your tormentor.

San Diego Probation Report, 2011

How it all began

March 1, 1988 was just another day and to Joan, at least, everything was as it should be. Joe was eleven, Jackie was nine and Juliann was four. Akira was busy working and Joan was happily cleaning pools part-time for a friend's business. Life was good. As was usual, Joe and Jackie walked themselves to school that day and Joan loaded her car with pool equipment and prepared for her cleaning route. She recalls:

> I dropped Juliann at preschool and finished my pool route within a few hours. The car needed a service, so I dropped it off at the mechanic's station near the house and walked home. It was pouring rain and I was absolutely soaked to the bone by the time I got home.
>
> I went straight to my master bathroom, undressed and began drying myself when Teddy, the family dog, started barking. She was in my bedroom and wouldn't stop barking. It was a ferocious bark and one that I had never heard from her before. I wrapped the towel around me and rushed into the bedroom to see what was wrong. And there he was. He was in my backyard with his hands wrapped around the handle of the sliding glass door. He was staring straight ahead and furiously shaking the door. Teddy was relentless and I was paralyzed in fear. I stood there trying to comprehend

what I was seeing. I looked from him, to Teddy, to the metal pin we used as an extra lock above the door. The pin was slowly sliding out as Lester shook and I knew he was going to get the door open.

I have no idea how long I stood and watched him, but he finally noticed me. For a brief moment we locked eyes and then he turned and ran. He jumped the fence into his own backyard and I was left there standing, clothed in nothing more than a towel and I couldn't catch my breath.

I stumbled to my bed and sat down. Teddy was finally silent and was staring at me as if to say, 'What now?' The crazy thing was, I had no idea. In all honesty, the first thought that had crossed my mind as I watched him shaking the door was 'If he wants to speak with me, why doesn't he come to the front door.' I was so naïve.

Ten minutes probably passed before I picked up the phone and rang a friend. I have no idea why I didn't call the police. No idea at all. But nothing like this had ever happened to me before and I suppose I didn't know what to do. My friend knew of Lester, she lived nearby and was witness to his usual antics from his balcony. All I remember her saying is 'Joan, you need to ring the police'. She probably said it a dozen times before I finally hung up with her and did just that.

When the Deputy Sheriffs arrived, Joan told them how she found Lester trying to break into her home. By the time they showed up, however, Lester was long gone. He may have suffered a self-diagnosed diminished IQ, but he certainly knew enough to flee the scene of his crime. An arrest warrant was issued, but the sheriffs would not locate him for several days.

Once the Deputy Sheriffs were gone, Joan was left alone to wade through a growing sea of emotions. She felt scared. She felt violated, helpless and angry. Then she remembered a number of peculiar, but seemingly innocuous things. For several months, she had noticed several pairs of panties going missing. She had assumed they were getting lost in the wash and didn't think much more of it. Washing for a family of five can be a tedious affair and it wasn't unusual for things to go missing. Several times she had also come home to find her back bedroom sliding door completely open: the very same door that Lester was just shaking. At the time, she thought that one of the kids must have left it open. But now, hit with a wave of panic and disgust, she realized that Lester could have been responsible for both.

Long after, Joan was tormented by visions of Lester in her home. She pictured him in her bedroom, rifling through her drawers and stealing her personal belongings. She wondered if he ever satisfied himself with a pair of her panties or a piece of clothing. But the question that troubled her the most was whether she had ever worn any of it after he had touched it.

It wasn't long after the attempted break-in that she first suffered what would become a painful recurring nightmare that would plague her for over two decades. In the dream, Lester slowly creeps down the long hallway to her bedroom where she is sleeping. He slowly draws towards her body and she can sense him, but she can not move. She is blindingly aware that he is next to her, but she can not scream. He quickly reaches out and wraps his hands around her neck and squeezes. She is completely paralysed in fear and pain and he keeps squeezing. The physical sense of the dream is so poignant that Joan eventually bolts awake and on each occasion is gasping for air and soaked in sweat.

Several days after his attempted break in, the sheriffs located Lester. He was formally interviewed, during which he provided his version of events. In summary, he claimed that he and a friend had been tossing a football in the street in front of Joan's house. He said the football was overthrown into her backyard so he jumped the fence to retrieve it. He claimed that once he was in her yard he heard Teddy (the family dog) barking. He said that he thought the dog wanted out of the house, so he was trying to open the door to be helpful. When the sheriffs asked him why he then ran off, he said that Joan had startled him.

There were obvious gaps and doubts in his story that left many questions unanswered. Why was he playing catch in the rain? Did he often let other people's dogs out of their houses? But perhaps most notably, why did he avoid the sheriffs for several days if he hadn't done anything wrong? But, Lester's story held with the sheriffs and they would later deliver the crushing blow to Joan that no criminal charges would be pursued.

In getting away with the attempted break in, Lester's confidence and indifference towards the law seemed to grow. Likewise, his obsession and aggression towards Joan increased substantially. This was the line in the sand—the turning point. Stalking wasn't even a recognized crime yet, but it seems this was undoubtedly the moment that Lester became a stalker.

Is anybody listening?

As with most suburban communities, it was hard to hide the fact that something had happened at the Eigner house. Most people are inherently inquisitive, but almost everyone wants to know if something criminal is occurring on their street. So it came as no surprise that the sight of police cars set the neighborhood abuzz with gossip. Joan rarely volunteered the information, but if asked, she would recount the ordeal. She was, however, cautious in sharing her story. She was embarrassed and scared of Lester's reprisal. But once she did, other people began regaling their own disturbing experiences with Lester. The following is a snapshot of their stories as they would later describe them to the prosecution team during the 1993 criminal trial.

Ming

Ming lived several houses from both Lester and the Eigners. Joan remembers her as a quiet woman who lived with her husband, who was an officer with the US military, and their young children. She described a night when two men, Lester and his friend, came to visit her husband's brother who was staying at her home while her husband was on deployment. Ming reported that the three men had been drinking alcohol for a while when she retired to her bedroom upstairs, leaving them to continue drinking in the downstairs kitchen. She stated that sometime later she was roused by a noise and woke to see Lester standing at the foot of her bed. His pants were reportedly around his ankles and he was masturbating. Ming claims that she screamed and Lester quickly fled the room.

Lester later claimed that the men had dared him to go upstairs and get into Ming's bed. This sort of testosterone and alcohol-fuelled challenge is easy to imagine, but it shouldn't justify Lester's actions that night. Fortunately for him, Ming never did report the matter to the Sheriff's Department. Perhaps she was too scared for her safety or the safety of her family, particularly with her husband away on deployment.

She was, however, prepared to testify for Joan in the 1993 trial and the prosecution team welcomed her support. But remarkably, Lester's attorney successfully argued that her evidence bore no relevance to Joan's case and the jury would never hear it. Despite showing a possible proclivity to sexual misconduct and deviance, the trial Judge found that Ming's testimony would be too prejudicial to Lester. It was quite unbelievable, but it was just one of the vagaries of California's justice system.

TOM

Tom and his wife also lived several houses from both Lester and the Eigners. They had three young daughters, all of whom were similar in age to Jackie and Juliann and attended the same school as the Eigner kids. Juliann in particular was very close with the two youngest children.

Like Ming, Tom provided a statement to the district attorney to support Joan's case in 1993, but his evidence was also prohibited at the trial. He reported that he regularly saw Lester yelling obscenities at passing cars and pedestrians; and described instances when Lester shouted sexual profanities at his wife and children, including a time when he witnessed Lester playing with his genitals while staring at them. The trial Judge stated that Tom's testimony was irrelevant to Joan's case because none of the behavior he described was directed at Joan or her family.

DORA AND JOHN

Dora and her family lived on the other side of the Eigners. They were a large and extended family. In her statement to the district attorney, she reported that Lester would make racial slurs against her and her family and described a time when her elderly father had to run and hide in their home after Lester tried to punch him in the face. She also claimed that Lester called her a 'bitch' and stared menacingly at her whenever she left her house. Her stepson, John, claimed that Lester would follow and chase him with his car and would yell racial outbursts at him and his family.

Despite living right next to each other, Dora's family and the Eigners were never particularly close. Joe and John were friends and would lift weights together or play catch in the front yard. Beyond that, however, the families were little more than friendly acquaintances. But like the other neighbors, Dora and John provided statements to the district attorney about their own experiences with Lester. But their evidence too was not admitted into court because it did not describe conduct directed at Joan.

CAROL

Carol had lived on the other side of Lester for a number of years. She and Joan weren't particularly close, but Joan was nonetheless grateful when Carol told her that Lester had allegedly bragged about swimming in the Eigners' pool. He apparently claimed to have done it when no one was home. Joan didn't know the veracity of the information, but having already caught Lester trying to break into her bedroom, she was inclined to believe it. The thought of Lester swimming in her pool repulsed her.

While it appeared that Joan had the confidence of most of her neighbors, she was still embarrassed when she explained that ultimately the Sheriff's Department didn't charge Lester with any criminal offence for his attempted break-in to her home. She felt as if their unwillingness to pursue the matter downplayed the seriousness of Lester's actions, or presented her as irrational or overdramatic.

This would be a feeling that Joan would become all too familiar with as Lester's harassment escalated to unfathomable proportions. This harassment would challenge Joan's strength of character and resolve in the face of inaction and disbelief.

What follows is a brief overview of the rampage of Lester's abuse and Joan's perceived failings of a justice system until one officer—Detective Howard Bradley from the San Diego Sheriff's Department—finally began to properly investigate her allegations. However, this would not occur for another five years, and it would take an attempted assault against Jackie to get any real help from the local Sheriff's Department. Until then, Joan was left to deal with the situation on her own.

Joan's nightmare

Reading by the pool, summer 1988

Not long after his attempted break-in to her home, Joan would again find Lester on her property. It was a warm day, the kids were at school, and the house was quiet. Joan decided to read by the pool, something she had often done before Lester's harassment began. But now, as she routinely did, she checked to see if Lester was home before heading outside. His car wasn't there so she thought it was safe. She put on her bathing suit, grabbed her book and quietly slipped into the backyard. Fortunately, the pool had been built on the north side of her home and out of view from Lester's property.

It wasn't long before Teddy began barking at the fence. Joan quickly jumped up and opened the gate to find Lester squatting on the ground. He had been peering through a crack in the fence at her and masturbating. She startled him when she appeared and both seemed unable to move for several surreal seconds. When she finally found her voice, she managed to scream 'get away'. He finally stood, hastily pulled up his pants and tore off towards his own backyard.

Disgusted and upset, Joan ran inside the house, got dressed and drove straight to the Sheriff's Station. She asked to make a complaint, but the officer on duty told her that there was nothing they could do.

She couldn't believe what she was hearing. First Lester got away with an attempted break in, now he would get away with indecent behavior. But the officer told her that Lester hadn't broken the law and that the next time it happened she needed to call the officers to her house, not come to the station. She felt sick at the thought of a 'next time.'

She pled with the officer, explaining that the reason she didn't call them to her house was because it always incited Lester further. She explained that every time Lester saw a police car at her home, his insults and threats only escalated. The officer offered no response and she returned home with an overwhelming feeling of isolation and despair.

Years later, in his motion to exclude this incident from evidence at the 1993 trial, Lester's attorney argued that it wasn't relevant to Joan's case and that there was no evidence that Lester's actions were directed at Joan. Remarkably, he even suggested that Joan was in fact invading Lester's privacy while he was masturbating.

> *Lester's Attorney:* Your honor, if I could address the court briefly. The masturbation issue, she—the witness—herself said from her own perception that he wasn't trying to get her attention. She put herself in a position to see that. Now to use this as a basis for some type of harassment or stalking charge I think is just—there's no link between the two. Especially when you're in a place you have a right to be, in your own privacy, that she puts herself in a position to see it. I submit ... he has a right to a certain amount of privacy also.

Amazingly, the Judge agreed. The Judge ruled to prohibit this evidence because it would be too prejudicial to Lester. The Judge believed the jury didn't need to hear about the incident to conclude Lester was harassing Joan. In ruling, the Judge stated:

> I think the witness had a right to be curious as to why the dog was barking and stand up and see what was going on. I think your argument was a very valid argument, but I will say that I think she does have a right to see what's going on, on her own property.

And as far as the not trying to get her attention, yes, there was a statement that she quite clearly said it was directed at her, but really not. I don't think something that she—it isn't to the same extent where he was out in the open doing this. I think it is evidence of harassment. Again, it would be a plan, and perhaps a motive in that the sexual satisfaction and viewing the lady becomes—kind of merge, but as of right now ... I am going to find that it will create a substantial danger of undue prejudice, confusing the issues. The issue is not whether he was masturbating. The issue would be whether the sexual comment, the comments that he made were sexual. And given the testimony, I don't think there's any doubt what a jury is going to conclude if the witness testifies, as she did here, that the threats were sexual. You don't need the conduct to explain what the threats were.

And the fact it was on her property, while it may be disputed—and assuming, because I have the evidence in that he was on her property, it's also in that he was essentially not exhibiting himself to her. Admittedly looking at her, but not—perhaps using her as a stimulus, but not dependent upon her seeing him for that stimulus. And so, as of right now, I would rule that out.

Staring Down the Barrel

On an otherwise normal autumn day Akira and Joe were raking leaves in the backyard, a tedious but normal chore. They hadn't been outside long when Lester walked out onto his second-story balcony to watch them. Akira paid him little attention until he realized that Lester was twirling a black handgun around his finger. Lester was smiling and looking directly at them. Akira yelled for Joe, who was only about twelve years old at the time, and they quickly went inside the house. Having had little success with the Sheriff's Department up until that point, Akira didn't bother to call them. He made sure Joe was okay, then made him promise not to tell his mother. Akira knew the stress that Joan was under; he had seen the changes in his wife and he wanted to tell her himself. That way, he figured, he could sanitize the seriousness of the incident and spare her from further anxiety. He would tell her that neither he nor Joe were overly troubled by Lester's behavior, knowing the thought of her kids being threatened could very well break her.

LESTER'S TAUNT

After his attempted break in, Lester began a litany of vulgar and threatening verbal abuse towards Joan. Virtually every time he saw her, he would call her a 'bitch' or 'cunt' and say things like 'I'm going to get you, whore', 'I'm going to fuck you' and 'Bend over for me, baby'. This was sometimes paired with Lester wiggling his tongue at her, grabbing his genitals or pretending to masturbate. It was repulsive, but it wasn't a crime. She was forced to suffer through. She cocooned herself and her kids the best she could and prayed Lester would disappear. It was the beginning of her social decline: one that would eventually see her trapped by feelings of helplessness and anxiety.

When Jackie became a teenager, Lester began directing the same behavior at her. He became a constant in her life as well and she grew to expect the harassment whenever she encountered him. There was certainly nothing normal about growing up like that, but it would spawn an ironic interest in crime and social justice—an interest that would steer her future studies and a subsequent career in law enforcement. At the time, it was difficult for Jackie to navigate her emotions. On the one hand, she was naturally afraid of Lester and the things he threatened to do, not only to her but to her mother as well. But on the other hand, she wanted to be strong for her mother. She knew that Joan was fighting to survive her own battle with Lester and didn't need to be burdened with her fear as well. It was a terrible position for any young person to be in.

It was around this time as well that Lester started tormenting Joan with the same song, over and over. When he was close enough so she could hear, he would whistle or sing the chorus of the 1969 hit *Smile a Little Smile for Me* by UK band Flying Machine. It turned her stomach every time she heard it. And to this day, it still does.

But perhaps his favorite gesture of all, and one he would use for the next twenty-three years, was pretending to shoot her. He would form his hand into the shape of a gun, take aim and mouth the word 'bang'. Years later, his mother, Gloria, would also adopt this move and direct it at Joan and many of her coworkers who happened past her house.

Lester also managed to obtain Joan's unlisted home phone number several times. For someone with a supposed diminished IQ, he was very clever when he wanted to be. At the height of his stalking, he rang the Eigners' home as many as twenty times a day. In one odd and telling exchange that occurred around Christmas of 1988, he said: 'Joan, this is Lester. Don't hang up. I wasn't trying to break into your house. I was just coming in to see you and I wish we could be friends.' In his world, maybe this is how friends behave.

When he called, he only had a voice for Joan. If the other Eigner members answered, they would only hear heavy breathing. When asked at trial how she knew it was Lester calling, she simply replied, 'Because he would tell me it was him.'

Indeed, part of the thrill was making her well aware of his desires. His outbursts over the phone didn't differ greatly from those he espoused in person. He would tell her what he thought of her and what he would like to do to her; and he would whistle or sing his chilling melody—*Smile a little smile for me*—over and over again.

Lester proved to be very resourceful when he wanted something bad enough. Much to Joan's frustration and amazement, he would continue to find her unlisted home phone number every time she changed it. As an example of his tenacity, he once tracked her number down through an ad that she placed in the *Auto Trader*—a sizable car sales publication.

She suspects that he saw the magazine's photographer taking pictures of the motorbike that Joe was selling. The ad featured in the publication the following week. That very day, he called her. When she answered the phone, he laughed in proud defiance and goaded, 'I found you!' For the next three days, he rang her constantly. She had to wait until the following Monday to change her phone number yet again.

Between 1988 and 1993 Joan changed her phone number at least three times. But this seemed only to amuse Lester. Each time he discovered it, he would taunt her by saying things like, 'You think you can run from me? You think you can hide from me?' By the end of this period, she didn't think she could. She couldn't escape this predator and she started to think that moving to another city was the only solution, something Akira wasn't prepared to do just yet.

During these five years, there were several periods of inactivity when Lester was very quiet. These lulls usually lasted for one or two months—just long enough to lure Joan into a false sense of hope. Then Lester would reappear and the threats and vulgarity would start all over again. The cycle was mentally and emotionally draining.

Into the Woods, 1988 to 1993

Joan had always been a fitness enthusiast with a particular passion for hiking. Like most working mothers, she relished the few moments she had for herself. She considered herself fortunate because of the variety of hiking trails available in and around Santee. But she would be forced to stop an activity that she loved and a freedom that most of us would take for granted after Lester began following her.

Several times he simply appeared when she was hiking a remote trail. Sometimes he would just stand there and stare at her while other times he would taunt her. She wouldn't feel safe to hike again until she bought a one hundred and twenty pound Rottweiler, Rhodesian Ridgeback cross in

1992. She named her Sadie and she would become a beloved member of the family and a fiercely protective watchdog.

It was clear that Lester had spent a substantial amount of time following Joan without her knowledge and had become familiar with her routines. He would also surface in other random places while Joan completed everyday errands. Life for Joan was quickly becoming untenable. She had to fight to do daily tasks and necessary domestic chores under the looming and growing threat of Lester's antics. Running down the street to buy groceries, pay a bill, or visit the bank was no longer something she could do as an ordinary part of life. These trips now required a complex decision making process that had to consider what Lester's movements might be.

In one rare exchange, Joan bravely spoke up and told Lester off. She generally preferred to ignore his antics, fearing a response would only spur him on. But not this day.

She had just finished her grocery shopping and was walking to her car when Lester rode his bike up next to her and said, 'Your ass is looking really good Joan.'

She tried to keep her voice from wavering and replied, 'You need to get a life.'

He laughed and told her that he had a life. He told her that the purpose of his life was to 'watch her ass.' He then told her to go home and tell Akira what he had said.

Vandalism

Joan experienced a number of random incidents of vandalism from the time she caught Lester trying to break into her bedroom. While she could never directly attribute them to him, she certainly had her suspicions and would later testify about these incidents at trial. They included a separate break-in to her garage, the destruction of fence boards, tree branches being ripped down, car tires being slashed and superglue being placed into the locks of her car. Interestingly, Lester would also be accused of putting superglue into the car locks of another woman years later.

THE PURSUIT

Beginning in mid 1992 and continuing until his arrest for stalking Joan in April 1993, Lester would follow her in his car on a near daily basis. It would become so frequent that it was common knowledge in the neighborhood.

The day that it first started was one Joan will never forget. She left home on her pool-cleaning route for the day. Ten minutes later, she arrived at her first scheduled cleaning and drove into the gated condominium complex. She navigated the narrow streets to the fenced pool, parked her car and went around the back to the small equipment room as she had many times before. But this time she noticed movement in the bushes only several feet away. The last thing she expected to see was Lester, but there he was. Like he had been when she caught him masturbating in her backyard, he was squatting down on his haunches and watching her. She felt as if her feet were nailed to the floor. She wanted to move but her body wouldn't respond. He never made a move towards her, but Joan could see the look of satisfaction on his face.

After what felt like ages, she ran from the dark equipment room and out to the relative safety of the open pool deck, where a man was sitting alone. Joan quickly approached him and begged him to stay while she cleaned the pool. The man stared at her, quite rightly confused, but he was happy to oblige. Within minutes, Lester appeared again. This time, he sat alone in his car next to the pool and watched her. He had clearly managed to defeat the automatic gates at the complex entrance.

The stranger was now suspicious of the situation so Joan explained that the 'man in the truck' had followed her there and that she was terrified of him. She again asked the stranger to stay while she finished the cleaning and he did. Perhaps disappointed that Joan wasn't alone, or perhaps satisfied with his efforts, Lester finally left. Joan stalled the cleaning as long as she could, then packed up the equipment and headed straight home. She was too scared to finish her route that day.

This was the moment that Joan realized Lester had been charting her movements beyond the immediate surroundings of her home. There was no other explanation. He had no other way of knowing her pool route, a rather complex schedule of cleanings that spread into suburbs up to thirty minutes away. This could mean only one thing: Lester had been following and plotting her movements for a long time. Most unnerving of all was that she had no idea that he had been lurking behind her that whole time. Indeed, she had always felt relatively safe when she worked, as it took her away from her home and his. Testifying about the start of all this, Joan stated:

> He would just be behind me. I would look in my rearview mirror and his car would be there and he followed me. I didn't want him to find out where the pools were so I would just go home ... On one occasion instead of going to the pool, I got on the freeway. I drove over to El Cajon. I was by the pool equipment store, so I thought I'm going to go ahead and go back here. There's a lot of people here and I'll just stay here for a while. I went in there. I was there for about twenty minutes. I came back out. I was driving down the street in El Cajon and he drove his truck coming the other way. He saw me and flipped a U-turn and started following me again ... so I just went back home.

She would eventually make it back home that day, but as soon as she parked her car Lester pulled into his driveway, got out of his truck and said: 'That was really fun, wasn't it?' Not long after, Joan was forced to quit her job.

Lester's pursuit of Joan would become more regular, ruthless, and eventually dangerous. Sometimes he would only follow her for minutes, other times for up to an hour. He would pace his car behind and alongside hers; he would laugh and wiggle his tongue at her; and several times he spat on her window. This eventually escalated to attempts to run her car off the road. What is worse, he would continue these exploits even after Joan began driving school buses full of disabled children. These incidents were so traumatizing that even today Joan can't stand to have a car pacing with her own.

Joan rang the Sheriff's Department on a number of occasions, but she was repeatedly told that they couldn't help her. They told her that there were no laws against driving on public roads. At one stage, Akira tried to stop Lester from following her. Dressed only in a bathrobe, he left the kids sleeping in their beds one morning and jumped into his car. He began chasing after Lester who was chasing after Joan. The three cars wound through suburban streets before Lester finally pulled over. Akira pulled up behind him, got out of the car and told Lester that this 'game' had to stop.

Akira later testified that Lester apologized that morning and actually stopped following Joan for about one month. Akira told the court that the cessation was probably more due to the fact that the Eigners went out of state for a four week vacation rather than Lester's conscience; because as soon as they returned home, Lester started following Joan again. It would take a very long time, but Lester was finally charged with Assault with a Deadly Weapon in April 1993 after one of his manic car chases.

JOAN TRIES TO TAKE ACTION

Lester's harassment had become so frequent and commonplace that Joan began to accept it as a part of her life. She was constantly told that there was nothing illegal about Lester's actions and that there was nothing the Sheriff's Department could do to stop it. His antics were well known within the neighborhood, but again there was nothing anyone could do to make him stop. By 1992, stalking had become criminalized in California and Joan wondered whether she could pursue a complaint. She discussed it with the Deputy Sheriffs at her local station and they told her that she would first need to obtain a restraining order, and he would need to breach that order before they could charge him with a crime. Like so many other stalking victims, Joan wondered if Lester was going to have to hurt her before the Sheriff's Department would do anything.

After four long years of enduring Lester's abuse and subsequent inaction by authorities, she thought she had just enough courage to fight for a restraining order. She asked the Sheriff's Department for the paperwork and took it home. She had no idea what any of it meant, she had no idea what she was getting herself into, and she was offered no assistance in completing it. For days, she simply stared at the application and considered the pros and cons of having a restraining order. In the end, she didn't file the application. She was too afraid of Lester's response and she didn't trust that the Deputy Sheriffs would protect her when she needed it. When questioned at trial why she didn't submit the paperwork at this stage, she replied:

> I did not get a restraining order because every time I would call the police or call the sheriffs, it made it worse. I was afraid the sheriffs weren't going to be there to back me, and when I got a restraining order things were going to get a lot worse.

Considering the lack of support and apathy shown to her for the past four years, it is no wonder she felt this way. Lester's track record demonstrated that any police intervention fueled his fury and harassment. It is a sad indictment on the justice system of the day that even with the existence of relevant laws, victims were unable to obtain the support that they needed.

Joan desperately tried to ignore Lester's harassment and to keep it out of her life and the lives of her children. For a while she recorded details of Lester's pursuits in a journal, but would eventually stop because the Sheriff's Department didn't seem interested in the absence of a restraining order. She didn't know what to do. She was living a nightmare, and at times she wanted to give up and let the fear, depression and anxiety swallow her up. She recalls:

> There were times when I was absolutely desperate; when I felt like I was just hanging on by my baby toenail.

She had become a prisoner in her own home. She wouldn't leave the house if she knew that Lester was home. She quit her pool cleaning job to minimize her exposure to his antics. Lester had even invaded her dreams. She had nightmares so horrific that she would grind and crack most of her teeth, later requiring major dental repairs that cost thousands of dollars; and she would suffer these nightmares for many, many years to come. She could no longer do even the mundane and routine things that most people take for granted. She desperately worried for her kids' safety and the damage that Lester's abuse was having on them and she fought to hide her fear and anxiety from them. Through tears, she later told the court what her life had become:

> I have locks on all my windows and doors and bolt locks. My children won't stay home alone ... I have a very large dog that goes everywhere I go ... I fear for my life and the life of my children ... I don't go out by myself. If he's anywhere around, I stay home ... I don't have anything left to give ... It just makes me nervous all the time ... I'm very short tempered and easily upset ... It doesn't take a lot to upset me because I'm nervous all the time. I worry about what might happen. I'm afraid to leave my children ... I've had nightmares that I've never had before ... I won't be out there if he's going to be around. I don't want him watching me.

Lester had invaded every aspect of her once pleasant and peaceful life. This was a life she and Akira had worked very hard to achieve, but the cracks in their marriage were starting to show. Joan knew she wasn't the carefree and attentive wife that she once was; and Akira didn't know how to help or counsel her. And as he began to pull away, her confusion and resentment only grew. They would try to make it work, but they both knew their marriage was dying.

THE FINAL STRAW

Joan knew she had little emotional resilience to survive the impact that Lester was having on her life. By now, Joe and Jackie were teenagers and Lester had begun harassing them as well. Akira bought her a handgun and she kept it loaded in the house. Everyday she wondered if that would be the day that she finally crumbled. That day would come on Valentines Day in 1993.

Lester's harassment was in full swing, but somehow Akira managed to get Joan out of the house to attend a dinner party at her local church. He never shared her religious devotion, but he thought she could use a change of scenery and the company of friends. She agreed to go, but made sure arrangements were made so the kids weren't home alone. Joe was three weeks shy of turning seventeen and he was going camping with his friends that night. Jackie was fourteen and her friend, Melanie, came over to stay with her. Juliann was nine and was sleeping over at a friend's house.

It was late afternoon and Joe was getting ready to leave for his camping trip. He, Jackie, Melanie and the Eigners' neighbor, John, were in the garage talking with the large paneled door open to the street. Soon after, Lester backed his car down his driveway and stopped in the street in front of them. He raised his hand outside his car window and pretended to shoot them.

Then he drove back onto his driveway and disappeared into his home. It was a creepy and bizarre thing to do, but it wasn't unusual by Lester's standards.

LESTER TARGETS JACKIE

Around seven o'clock, Jackie and Melanie left to get dinner. They went through the back yard gate and walked down the embankment to the intersection below, where they crossed over Mast Boulevard to the taco shop at the small strip mall across the street. The embankment, the intersection and the strip mall were all easily visible from Lester's backyard. The girls made it to the shop and ordered their food without any trouble. But when they went back outside to wait for their order, they heard a familiar voice shouting and whistling at them. They looked up and saw Lester standing on his balcony laughing at them. Frightened, they went back inside the shop.

Several minutes later, the girls took their food to go and walked back outside. With Lester nowhere in sight, the girls headed back to the Eigners' home. They waited at the same intersection that they had crossed before and when the pedestrian crossing light turned green, they started across the street. They made it about halfway when they both saw Lester's car racing toward them. It all happened so quick, but with surreal clarity. Melanie asked Jackie 'Is that Lester?' Jackie shouted back 'Yes!' and shoved Melanie onto the sidewalk before diving onto the cement herself. The whine of Lester's engine squealed as he tore past them. Both girls would later testify that they believed his car had come within five feet of striking them.

Shaken and disoriented, the girls scurried a few yards up the Eigners' embankment and hid behind a small bush. From there, they saw Lester do a U-turn and return to the same intersection. His car came to a slow stop at the red light. He leaned his head out of the driver's side window and stared at the girls. He began waving to them and was laughing.

Scared and breathless, Jackie and Melanie huddled together. They were trying to make sense of what was happening. At that moment, a familiar vehicle stopped at the traffic lights in front of them. They raced to the van and frantically tried to open the rear sliding door. The male driver—a close friend of Joe's—yelled to them that the handle was broken. They still pounded the windows and pulled at the door handle, but to no avail. They looked over helplessly at Lester, who was watching their fear with growing delight.

Just then, another car pulled up and a female passenger yelled for the girls to get in. Unbelievably, a classmate and her boyfriend (Jennifer and Javier) had watched the entire event transpire. They saw Jackie and Melanie crossing the street; saw Lester race his vehicle at them; saw the terrified girls hiding in the bushes; and watched as Lester turned his vehicle around to taunt them. The girls jumped into the backseat of Javier's car and when his light turned green, he tore away from the intersection. Jennifer and Javier would both later testify that the girls were frantic and kept repeating: 'he was trying to hit us!' While they had no idea who *he* was, they knew the girls were in trouble and knew they had to get help. For the next few minutes, Lester chased after Javier's car. Javier would eventually lose Lester and return the girls safely back to the Eigners' home.

The girls rushed into the house and through tears they told Joe and John what had happened. By now, other friends of Joe's had arrived for their camping trip. Everyone suggested that they should ring the Sheriff's Department, but in the end, it was John that dialed. He spoke with an operator and requested a uniformed officer attend to take a report of Lester's terrifying and near deadly assault. The operator asked him to provide the license plate number of the vehicle Lester had been driving so one of Joe's friends went to check. A few seconds later he burst back into the house. He was visibly scared and said he had heard someone hiding in the bushes in Lester's front yard. With strength in numbers, they all crept into the garage and listened. They could all hear the bushes rustling and knew Lester must have been hiding there. So they all returned to the house to wait for the Deputy Sheriff.

The Deputy Sheriff arrived a short time later. The group immediately told him Lester was hiding in the bushes, but John would later testify that the officer didn't initially believe them. The group persisted and the officer finally retraced his earlier steps past Lester's front yard, but this time he used his flashlight to check the surrounds. Within seconds, he found Lester lying in the bushes. Lester quickly complied with the officer's commands to stand up. When he did, a long diving knife was clearly visible in his back pocket. Lester told the officer that he was waiting for Joe who he claimed had been vandalizing his car and slashing his tires. But when the officer inspected Lester's car, there was no damage.

The officer later testified that Lester was so well hidden in the bushes that he had walked right past him when he first arrived onsite. He said Lester was 'lying down ... he was completely concealed in the bushes, not squatting, not sitting'. When asked whether Lester appeared to be joking when he said he was waiting to get Joe, the officer replied 'No, Ma'am. I didn't find any humor in his voice or anything to indicate that he was being jovial in any manner'.

The officer returned to the Eigners' garage and listened to Jackie and Melanie. It was clearly a harrowing experience for both the girls as they fought tears and told their story with wavering voices, but the officer simply told them that there was nothing he could do. He explained that Lester was on his property, that he was legally entitled to carry the knife, and that he hadn't committed a crime. Despite the night's events, and his admission of intent to attack Joe, Lester wouldn't be arrested that night.

As the officer left her house that night, Jackie's heart sank in disbelief and bewilderment. She would later testify that she truly thought Lester had tried to kill her.

It wasn't long after the officer left when Lester came back to the Eigners' garage looking for another fight. Joe and his friends were still there and Lester shouted to him, 'Your mom gives good head. I'm going to get you.'

When Joe didn't retaliate, Lester jumped into his car and drove off. Not long after, the boys left for their camping trip and the girls—too afraid to stay at the house alone—arranged to go to another friend's house until Joan and Akira got home.

Around ten o'clock that evening Joan and Akira returned home to a dark and empty house. Jackie had left a message for them on the home answering machine. She told her parents where she was and said that Lester had tried to run her and Melanie over. She said that a Deputy Sheriff had been out to the house, but that she would explain what had happened when they came to pick her up. Horrified and frantic, Akira raced out and brought Jackie home.

Without pausing for breath, and choking back sobs, she told them exactly what happened. She told them how she thought she was going to be killed and how the Deputy Sheriff explained that there was nothing he could do. It was a heart-wrenching story for a mother to hear, and Joan tried her best to stay composed for her daughter. When Jackie finished, Joan rang the Sheriff's Department and demanded assistance. They told her that they wouldn't come back to her house because they had already taken the report. She pleaded with them to return and arrest Lester but they refused.

ENTER DETECTIVE BRADLEY

Lester had finally gone too far. He had gone after one of Joan's kids. That was her final straw. As it was, she was barely able to survive the ruthless harassment herself, but directing his vicious insanity at her kids was intolerable. In a rage of maternal anger and gutting helplessness, Joan collapsed into sobs and began to steel herself for what she had to the following morning.

So the next day I went down to the station and I remember I was just livid. I was just fit to be tied. I was so angry, I was so upset. This had been going on for so long. He had nearly killed one of my kids and I couldn't get any help. This is when they sent Howard Bradley out and, if I recall correctly, he told me that when I came in, they all sort of laughed and said, 'It's that crazy lady again.' And he said he would go and talk to 'her' this time.

It would become a decision that would change Detective Bradley's life, but it was also a case that was close to home, as he had three young children of his own at the time. It would also become a case that he was proud to have worked on. He would closely follow Joan's case over the ensuing years and attend subsequent hearings and trials to support her and her family. In 1994, Joan would give Detective Bradley a small memento—a knight made of metal—as a token of her sincere gratitude for his care and persistence. She would tell him that he was her 'knight in shining armor'. If you were to go see Detective Bradley today, you would find this knight proudly resting on his desk. It is a reminder for him of the outstanding work he did in securing one of California's first non-familial stalking convictions.

Rather than disdain, impatience and disbelief, Detective Bradley was the first officer to meet Joan's pleas for help with care, concern and diligence. He was the first officer to take her and her allegations seriously. It is quite remarkable, but he was also the first officer to come up to the Eigners' home, sit down and talk to all the family members and attempt to find out what was really going on. It didn't take long to convince Detective Bradley that Joan and her family were in grave danger. He advised her to get a restraining order immediately.

TAKING ACTION

Joan feared what retribution a restraining order would provoke, but she was more afraid of what would happen if she did nothing at all. Lester had gone after one of her kids and she had no doubt he would try again. With Detective Bradley's support, she applied for a temporary restraining order, which was served on Lester on March 7, 1993. As she feared it would, it sent Lester into a frenzy of anger. The very next day, he burst out of his front door as she was arriving home with her kids. He pulled out a camera, started taking pictures of them, and called Joan a 'bitch.'

By now, Joan had also started to seek legal counsel from a family friend, Attorney Charles 'Chuck' Nachand. He agreed to assist Joan in her criminal matters and initiate civil proceedings against Lester if Joan wished. Chuck told her that he would help her in any way that he could to get rid of Lester.

On March 9, 1993, he filed a civil complaint against Lester on Joan's behalf that would take five long years of legal battles and appeals to resolve. It wouldn't be until 1998 that Joan would have a remarkable win that held huge significance not only for her and her family, but for the legal community as well. The significance of this civil case is discussed in further detail in the next chapter.

On March 10, 1993, with the support of Akira and Chuck, Joan attended her hearing at the San Diego Superior Court. A novice with the justice system and keenly adverse to confrontation, she found it unfair and incredibly difficult to sit near Lester and watch the man she had grown to fear and detest. She prayed it would end quickly. She listened to Chuck tell of the countless reasons why the law should intervene to protect her and her kids. Lester presented a completely different version of events, claiming it was actually Joan who was harassing him, before unashamedly seeking a cross temporary restraining order against her.

After hearing evidence from both sides, the Judge ruled in Joan's favor and denied Lester's request. But, instead of curbing his conduct, the restraining order only served to intensify Lester's hate and harassment of Joan. Joan recalls:

> I can't even explain the feeling of relief that I had when the hearing was over. I remember just sitting down and sobbing because my emotions were so intense. I was just a nervous wreck. I remember just falling apart and crying in the chair after it was all over and shaking. And I remember thinking 'Ok, this is over, I have done what I needed to do. It's going to stop. Problem solved.' But of course it wasn't. The very next day I was out for a walk and here he comes. He came right up behind me and started taunting me, making his sexual comments and saying, 'I'm going to kill you, you fucking bitch.'
>
> I called the Sheriff's Department and they came out and I filed a restraining order violation. It was literally not even a day later. And of course I am thinking they would go arrest him. And of course they didn't. They talked to him and told him that he couldn't do those things. This happened two or three more times before Detective Bradley finally took it to the District Attorney's office and tried to get them to press charges for a restraining order violation. Things started to escalate even more, and at one point Lester even threatened

Detective Bradley. Lester told him, 'I know where your wife shops, I know where your kids go to school.' It was after this that I started to get real help from the Sheriff's Department and the District Attorney's office—because it became a real personal problem for them.

Despite repeated violations of his restraining order, Lester wasn't arrested or charged. The message must have seemed quite clear to him that the restraining order was really just a piece of paper. So he continued.

On April 14, 1993, he again followed her, this time while she was walking in the local foothills. By now, she had her new watchdog Sadie and she felt confident to resume walking under her protection. Sadie was the first to hear Lester behind them that day and she stood perfectly still as he approached. Joan followed the dog's gaze and saw Lester fast approaching on his bike. He wasn't game enough to come very close with Sadie there, but he got close enough to yell, 'You have three months to move. Bend over, baby,' before riding off. Joan went home and immediately called the Sheriff's Department. Lester had once again violated his order, but he would not be charged.

The following day, Lester decided to up the ante. When Joan left for work at approximately six o'clock, Lester was on his driveway and standing next to his car with the engine running. When he saw Joan come outside, Lester stepped towards her and said 'Joanie, Joanie, smile a little smile. Three hundred dollars. You're going to pay.' Joan got into her car and drove off. She would only get a few blocks from home when she looked into her rearview mirror and saw Lester's car racing up behind her. He followed her for miles, veering his car at hers and forcing her to swerve off the road a number of times. At one stage, he was so close to her car that he spat on her passenger side window.

This new crime of stalking was either too hard or too difficult to investigate and prosecute. Joan and her family seemed to be on their own. The Deputy Sheriffs would repeatedly tell her: 'He is not breaking any laws';

'You haven't been assaulted'; 'There's nothing we can do about it'. But at long last, the justice system finally seemed to be working in her favor. Later that day, Lester was arrested and charged with Stalking and Assault With a Deadly Weapon.

Finally, Joan had some results. But Lester was far from finished. Only days after his arrest, he rode his bike to an intersection located about half a mile from Joan's work. Who knows how long he had been waiting for her, but at eleven-forty, Joan spotted him. It was too late for her to stop or change direction, so she was forced to drive right past him. Not wanting to miss an opportunity, Lester opened his mouth and wiggled his tongue at her. Joan continued on her way and reported the incident to the Sheriff's Department when she got home.

Three weeks later on May 10, 1993, Lester would appear yet again near Joan's work. Still accustomed to varying her routines to avoid him, Joan left for work about thirty minutes early. She was almost to work when she spotted him on the opposite side of the road. He was on his bike and very far from home. She knew the only reason he was there was to find her. As they passed each other, he made his hand into the shape of a gun, pointed it directly at Joan and mouthed the word 'Bang.' Joan went directly to work and reported the incident to the Sheriff's Department. Lester was subsequently charged with violating his restraining order.

Stroke of genius

There is nothing like the peace of mind and feeling of security that comes from having a big and defensive dog at your side. Joan and Akira bought Sadie in 1992, at the height of Lester's harassment. Teddy, the previous family dog, had since died and Joan needed a new protective companion. They searched the classified ads and found a litter of Rottweiler, Rhodesian Ridgeback cross pups that looked promising. Joan rang up to enquire and was told that both parents were large for their breed so she was intrigued. The family drove out the following weekend and Sadie was the first puppy to greet them as they arrived. From the very first day that they met her, Sadie was an inquisitive and staunch girl. At just eight weeks old and already weighing a whooping thirty pounds, Joan was convinced that this was the right dog for her. Sadie would grow into a one hundred and twenty pound fiercely protective and loving member of the family. For Joan, Sadie brought her new confidence to get out and she took the dog everywhere. She loved that Sadie had zero interest in socializing with anyone, person or canine; and still marvels that it was probably Sadie's outright aggression that would lead her to Attorney Chuck Nachand and a successful civil lawsuit that no one would have dreamed possible.

Joan had been taking Sadie to Jackie's soccer games for some time and her size and protective demeanor aroused the curiosity of many other spectators. One in particular was Chuck, an Attorney who had his own law practice in northern San Diego. Chuck's daughter played on the same team as Jackie and the families had met earlier that season. He had seen Sadie several times before he finally asked Joan why she had such a big dog. Moreover, a dog that wasn't just overly protective, but was downright hostile to anyone that came near Joan or her kids.

Without thinking, Joan poured her heart out to Chuck. She told him everything about Lester and the stalking: the threats, harassment, and the ineffectual criminal justice system. Chuck simply told her that she didn't have to live like that. He promised to help her saying: 'We'll sue, we'll put it in the newspaper, we'll do what we have to do to get them to help you.'

The United States is often criticized because its legal system features more lawsuits than any country in the world. Lawyers work tirelessly encouraging and assisting people to sue one another, sometimes for the most trivial matters. But in this case the system is not necessarily a bad thing. In fact for Joan and her family, while it would be a painstakingly slow process, this was the first tangible assistance that she had received from the legal system.

In March 1993, Chuck devised a plan to help Joan through a civil law suit. She would sue Lester and his mother for damages for stalking, as well as assault, hate crimes, harassment, invasion of privacy, obscene, threatening or annoying telephone calls, and general negligence.

The genius in his plan was that the Eigners would seek damages from an insurance company, not the Worthington family. Because Lester was living with his mother, Chuck believed that a claim for damages could be made against Gloria's insurer, State Farm Fire and Casualty (State Farm). Gloria had a mortgage, so she was required to have a home and contents insurance policy. A home and contents insurance policy has two basic components: property protection and protection against personal liability. Personal liability protection means that you are legally obligated to pay money to another person for actions caused by the person with the insurance, their family, and their property.

Chuck's argument boiled down to one key point: Gloria had failed to control Lester's actions and had, in effect, allowed the harassment and stalking to continue from her property. This caused the Eigners to suffer physical injury, emotional distress and property damage. This meant that there was a claim for damages that was potentially covered under the State Farm homeowner's policy.

Gloria Worthington sent the claim to State Farm. They denied the claim outright, as they believed that there was no basis to it and that they had no duty to defend the lawsuit. State Farm conducted no investigation beyond a reading of the case and argued in a letter to Gloria Worthington that after 'very careful review ... there was no potential for coverage because the policy excluded damages arising out of the use of an automobile, and the complaint alleged no other bodily injury or property damage'.

The letter's closing paragraph stated, 'We, of course, are willing to consider any further documentation or information with regard to the issues presented. We request that any supplemental information ... be forwarded to us for consideration.'

With State Farm rejecting the claim, the Eigners proceeded to take action in a trial. Prior to the trial commencing, the Judge told Chuck that he was concerned about aspects of the case and that he would visit Lester in prison. When the visit was over, the Judge rang Joan and asked her to meet with him in his chambers. Naturally concerned, she said that she would and drove straight over.

The Judge told her that his own daughter had been stalked by an ex-boyfriend and that he understood the horror of this kind of behavior.

He said that he thought he could talk some sense into Lester but instead formed the belief that Lester truly wanted to kill Joan. He urged her to be careful, then gave instructions that Lester was never to be present in his courtroom.

At the trial, Joan and her family would finally tell their story. At last, Lester's remorseless, relentless, and terrifying conduct was placed on the record for all to see.

During the trial, Joan testified about how the harassment had caused her to lose sleep, vomit, develop a skin condition and sustain neck and muscle strains and scratches from nightmares where she was 'trying to get away from Lester'. Every member of Joan's family had suffered some type of physical or emotional injury as a result of Lester's conduct and by 1997 the family's medical bills were approximately nineteen thousand dollars.

Gloria presented no evidence or argument. The Judge found that Gloria had been negligent and awarded the Eigners damages in the amount of $240,700. The judgment included an award for property damage and reimbursement of the family's medical bills for the physical injuries suffered by Lester's conduct.

Since the judgment included an award for bodily injury and property damage covered under its homeowner's policy, State Farm moved to vacate the judgment. They argued that if it had known of the potential coverage, it would have defended the action and likely obtained a different result. The trial court denied the motion, concluding that the insurer should have conducted an investigation based on the allegations of the complaint where it would have learned that it had a duty to defend. State Farm appealed the decision to the California Court of Appeal but lost. The appeals court observed: 'A liability insurer owes a broad duty to defend its insured against claims that create a potential for indemnity. The carrier must defend a suit which potentially seeks damages within the coverage of the policy.'

The Court of Appeal found that State Farm produced no evidence that it conducted any investigation whatsoever as to the nature of the Eigners' claims other than reading the complaint before refusing to defend. State Farm could have, but did not, contact the Eigners' Attorney regarding the 'nature, type or style of damages being requested by the plaintiffs'. If State Farm had contacted Chuck, they would have learned of the physical injuries suffered by Joan in trying to get away from Lester and that she required medical treatment. State Farm would also have learned of the property damage committed by Lester.

While the tables had begun to turn on Lester, it was also a turning point in relation to the duties of insurance companies: insurers have a positive duty to investigate the facts giving rise to a lawsuit to determine if a potentially covered claim may result.

The irony was that the awarding of monetary damages was a bonus. Chuck had never launched the civil action to obtain money. The objective was only ever to make Lester stop from engaging in his criminal conduct. While the Eigners would not actually see any of the awarded money until 1998, Chuck's five year battle and subsequent victory was unheralded. Neither Chuck nor the wider legal fraternity could believe the court had ruled in Joan's favor. And, as any online search engine shows, *Eigner v Worthington* would set the precedent for many other civil actions to come.

HUNG JURY

THE PRELIMINARY HEARINGS

In the US, a preliminary hearing (evidentiary hearing) is a proceeding held to determine whether there is enough evidence to require a trial. Witnesses are called to answers questions before a Judge, who must find probable cause that a crime was committed. If a Judge determines that there is sufficient evidence to proceed to trial, the court schedules an arraignment, at which the defendant will enter a plea. If that plea is not guilty, the prosecution will continue and a trial date is set.

In June 1993, two separate preliminary hearings would be held for the matter of the People of the State of California vs. Lester L. Worthington. The first of these hearings presented the case against Lester regarding his attempt to run Jackie and Melanie over with his car. The second was held to present the case against Lester regarding his stalking of Joan, his attempt to run her off the road, and several violations of his restraining order.

Representing the People (Joan and her family) was a Deputy District Attorney. Representing the Defendant (Lester) was a public defender. In total, only five witnesses would be called: Joan, Tom (Joan's neighbor), a Deputy Sheriff, Detective Howard Bradley, and Lester. Joan would detail

Lester's conduct over the past five years and explain how it had subsequently altered her life. In her closing arguments, the Deputy District Attorney summed it up as follows:

> What we have here is an individual that, based upon an incident five years ago—breaking into somebody else's house—has decided that that person deserves to be harassed for the rest of their born days. The perfect line that came out in testimony today is exactly what this defendant wants to do is to watch Joan Eigner. The line at the Vons store, 'My life is watching you', and that's what his life is.
>
> She gets a restraining order because he nearly runs her daughter over ... This man is now going after her children. She gets a restraining order but that doesn't stop it. In fact, that increases the abuse ... Repeated harassment day after day after day ... There is no way to describe what this defendant did. What he did wasn't in fun. What he did wasn't in jest. Trying to hit another car while it's travelling down the roadway is not in fun or in jest. Going to her place of work, heading up on his bike towards her place of work knowing there's a restraining order and continuing to violate it. We have heard from Ms. Eigner that it's just gotten worse. It's not getting better. He hasn't stopped. He's not going to stop.
>
> That he made a credible threat. He tried to run her off the road. He tried to run her daughter off the road. He's found in the bushes with a knife, saying he's going to 'get' her oldest son. He wants to fight with these people. He wants to hurt these people. There's a credible threat there and Joan Eigner is very scared ... it's affected her home life. It's affected her work. She's lost one job because of this guy.

The hearings were relatively swift. The Judge found that there was sufficient evidence for four counts of criminal conduct, including Stalking, Assault With a Deadly Weapon, and two counts of violating his restraining order. An arraignment was scheduled for July 12, 1993. The Deputy District Attorney would ask the Judge to remand (hold) Lester in custody unless he could post a fifty thousand dollar bail. She argued that he posed an even greater threat to Joan now that he was going to trial. Her summation painted a bleak picture for Joan:

> ... the People would be asking at this time that the Defendant be remanded into custody on $50,000 bail. In citing for that I will cite to the court the events leading up to the stay-away order.
>
> Once this case was filed and once the case on the daughter, Jackie Eigner, was filed, it still did not deter Mr. Worthington. Mr. Worthington has been, in the past few weeks, at the youngest daughter's school, standing there waiting for her.
>
> He has made comments to Detective Bradley, citing a week ago last Thursday, he called him 'a dick-head' in the courthouse, not out on the street, but here. Last Thursday we are in court for the preliminary hearing and he calls Detective Bradley a 'fucking fuck-head' in the courthouse, standing before a Judge who is going to hear his preliminary hearing. He doesn't care. He gives Detective Bradley the finger in the courtroom. He has glared at Joan Eigner, made it a specific point to walk out in the hallway to stand in front of her to glare, not just a coincidental contact but to do these things here in our courthouse ... He was removed from the area for that purpose ... The People feel he's a serious threat, especially in light of the bind-over. He seems to be a loose cannon. What seems to happen is after every little court appearance he does something else, and this is the biggest one so far.'

At his arraignment, Lester pleaded not guilty and his criminal trial was scheduled.

THE TRIAL

On November 9, 1993, the People of the State of California vs. Lester L. Worthington began in the Superior Court of the State of California— El Cajon Branch. The matter was heard before a Superior Court Judge. The Deputy District Attorney that prosecuted the preliminary hearing would again represent the People and attorneys would represent Lester.

As with many criminal trials in the US, this one began with the presentation of evidence to the Judge so she could determine which portions of testimony she would permit. This process usually takes place in the early stages of a trial and is conducted outside the presence of the jury. Witnesses give their evidence before the Judge and counsel (the prosecution and defense). The Judge then makes an ultimate ruling that is quite frankly one of the great paradoxes of criminal prosecution. In effect, the jury will not get to hear 'the truth, the whole truth and nothing but the truth'—the oath a witness is made to swear. Instead, the jury will only hear that testimony which the Judge does not feel will be 'too prejudicial' towards the accused. This often includes, for instance, details of an accused's criminal history. This is something the courts treat very seriously. In fact, trials have been aborted after details of an accused's previous convictions have been leaked to the public.

While this process is in place for good reason, it has some weaknesses. An enormous amount of responsibility is placed on a trial Judge to strike a balance that ensures equity for both sides and will present an accurate picture for the jury so they can deliver an informed, fair and just verdict. But it certainly doesn't seem fair that a jury can hear favorable reports and good character references about an accused, but isn't allowed to know certain adverse details about their past.

At the outset of the trial, Joan was instructed not to raise a number of issues in her testimony. Unfortunately, those facts would have provided the jury with critical insights into Lester's deviant demeanor. This included the time she found him masturbating at her back fence, the time Ming found him masturbating in her bedroom, and admissions of his frequent drug use. Other excluded evidence included:

- The fact that Joan's vehicle had been vandalized, including punctured tires and the insertion of super glue in her locks.

- Details of Lester's proficiency in martial arts and regular attendance at martial arts school. The Defense successfully argued that Lester's knowledge and skills in martial arts did not suggest or show that he was a violent person. But Lester would often use public displays of his martial arts practice—for example, swinging nunchucks in his garage—as a way to intimidate the Eigners. In fact, he would later admit under oath that he had lied about holding a black belt in order to scare both Detective Bradley and the Eigners.

- Evidence by neighbor Tom about Lester's behavior towards his wife and daughters. This included Lester yelling profanity, making obscene gestures and touching his genitals while staring at his daughters.

- Evidence by neighbor Dora that Lester intimidated her. This included calling her a 'bitch' and 'staring her down' when she left her home, attempting to punch her elderly father and threatening her stepson.

- Evidence by neighbor John that Lester intimidated his family. This included following him in his vehicle on numerous occasions, yelling racial slurs and trying to pick a fight with his elderly grandfather.

It matters little now whether the admission of this evidence would have altered the jury's verdict. But at the time, it was something Joan found incredibly unfair and challenging. Having no previous exposure to the justice system, she felt like an outsider. When the Judge instructed her not to speak about issues that she felt were important to her case, she wanted to make her objections known. But it was made quite clear to her that opposition in any form would not be tolerated. While the District Attorney genuinely wanted to help her, Joan held little confidence in the system that she thought was there to protect people like her. Victims of crime describe this feeling time and time again, and research shows this to be a major factor for not reporting their victimization to authorities.

THE PEOPLE'S CASE

The prosecution called ten witnesses for the People's case. This included evidence from most of the Eigner family members—the exception being Juliann who was only ten years old at the time. Instead, Joan gave testimony about the incidents that involved her youngest daughter, including times when Lester took photographs of Juliann and threatened to choke and kill her. Joe and Jackie were only seventeen and fifteen years old at the time, but they would take the stand on behalf of their mother, in a show of courage and maturity beyond their years.

Joan's testimony would span the entire five year period, from the attempted break-in in 1988 to Lester's most recent restraining order breach in May 1993. She would be on the stand over the course of two days and would answer a total of nine hundred and eighty-seven questions. This would mark the first and toughest of many court appearances in which Joan would have to plead her case. Throughout her testimony, she visibly shook, cried, and had to request several short recesses to gather her composure. She felt openly mocked by the Defense attorney and was portrayed as a pathological liar.

She was made to defend and repeat her claims, but was often cautioned by the Judge for providing more information than was necessary to answer the original question. At one stage, the Defense Attorney moved for a mistrial, claiming that there was improper conduct by the District Attorney's office in failing to properly caution Joan about issues that she could not discuss on the stand. In an ensuing sidebar (a discussion outside the presence of the jury), Lester's attorney claimed Joan intentionally raised topics outside the scope of questioning. He then stated, 'You can tell what kind of witness she is. She is so excited to testify she just starts running at the mouth.'

Joan was hardly excited to be the target of Lester's attention. She was even less excited to be sitting in a courtroom talking about it. While the Judge did not challenge the attorney's audacity, she was quick to deny his motion. She pointed out that any perceived misspeak on Joan's part was more likely due to apprehension than malice. She then highlighted the fact that they had just abandoned Joan in the courtroom with her accused stalker. As an amateur with the justice system, Joan found the process incredibly confusing and frustrating. As a victim, she found it offensive. She felt demonized as the Defense tried to weaken her credibility. She felt cheap like she was begging for each juror to believe her.

Joan's parents faithfully attended court every day for their daughter. Their show of support was bittersweet for Joan. Even now she finds it difficult to recount the effects her testimony had on them, as she was forced to repeat the numerous vulgarities that she was subjected to and watch helplessly as her father silently wept at the back of the courtroom. A strong and unflappable man, Joan had never seen her father cry.

Akira testified about the frequency of Lester's harassment of his wife. He would say that while Lester clearly thought his torment of Joan was a game, that Joan definitely did not view it that way. He spoke about the changes he saw in his wife, including an increased anxiety and nervousness that affected her daily life. He told how they were forced to do things they would not have otherwise considered, like locking the doors when they were home. Lastly, he detailed how the years of Lester's harassment had torn Joan down and created a tension in their marriage.

Joe testified about the time Lester pointed a handgun at him and Akira and about the night Lester tried to run Jackie and Melanie over. He explained how straight after the Deputy Sheriffs left their house that night, Lester came outside and shouted to him that Joan 'gives good head.' He testified that, prior to this incident, Lester had threatened him on at least five occasions. These threats usually involved Lester forming his hand into the shape of a gun and pretending to shoot Joe, or telling him that he was going to 'get' him. Joe denied the Defense's allegations that there was an ongoing feud between himself and Lester, or that Joe provoked Lester's harassment.

Jackie's testimony largely concerned the night Lester tried to run her and Melanie down. She detailed the events for the jury, stating that she believed Lester came within five feet of striking them with his vehicle. She told them that she believed he would have done so if they had not jumped out of the way. Jackie remained strong during her testimony, breaking down into tears only when she described her fear when Lester came out of the bushes with a long knife and told the Deputy Sheriffs he was going to use it on her brother. Jackie recalls:

> It was over two decades ago, but I still remember. The corridors of the courthouse were crowded, dirty and loud. I was scared, I was so young and I felt terribly alone. Even though the Deputy District Attorney tried to prepare me, I had no idea what awaited me in that courtroom. But I knew Lester was in there. I knew I would have to sit near him. I didn't want him to look at me, and I didn't want to look at him. I remember Mel was shaking. Our friendship would never be the same after this whole ordeal, which was something I have always regretted. She was a warm and funny girl and I considered her to be a close friend at the time. But I really don't blame her for distancing herself from me after being dragged through my family's dramas and the terror of testifying. It is certainly never easy for anyone, but I can still

remember her bursting out of the courtroom in tears and racing past me in the corridor. Barred from communicating, I couldn't even console her.

I was finally called into the courtroom. Lester was smiling as I was sworn in. I took my seat in the witness box and began my testimony. I tried hard to be brave, but I found it incredibly difficult to face him. I was asked to identify him to the court and I can still see his greasy and unkempt hair. I can still picture the bemused look on his face. I just wanted to run: run from him, his condescending attorneys and the expressionless stares of the twelve jurors. I could hear my voice wavering throughout my testimony and I chided myself for it. I didn't want to look weak and it certainly didn't help when I looked at my grandparents—people we associate with strength, experience and resolve—who just looked utterly lost and sad.

The Defense attorney tried to humiliate and undermine my testimony. At fifteen years of age it is hard to understand that this was just part of his job. As he called into question the veracity of my claims and openly displayed his disbelief, I hated him. Every time he cut me off or objected to my answers, I wanted to scream. At one point he came so close to me that I could see the pores on his nose. I wanted to be there for my mom, but I couldn't wait to get off the stand.

Several neighbors would testify about the regularity of Lester's harassment of Joan. They would say it was common knowledge that Lester followed Joan in his car, and that every morning around six o'clock, the engine to Lester's car would be running. They said he would be waiting nearby and would jump into his car and chase after Joan as soon as she left for work.

Jackie's friends, Melanie, Jennifer and Javier, testified about the night Lester tried to run Jackie and Melanie down. Melanie struggled to stifle sobs through most of her testimony as she described what happened. Jennifer and Javier testified that they saw the entire event unfold and then described the chase that ensued after the girls jumped into Javier's car. Despite their age, both witnesses provided compelling and confident testimony.

Lastly, the Deputy District Attorney called the Deputy Sheriff who attended the Eigners' home after Lester's attempt to run the girls down. He provided clear and uncontroversial testimony. He described how he found Lester hiding in the bushes with a hunting knife and how he believed Lester's threat to Joe was not made in jest.

The People then rested their case.

THE DEFENSE'S CASE

As the People's case came to a close, Lester's Defense attorneys prepared their first move—a motion for an acquittal. Within minutes of the Deputy District Attorney wrapping up her case, the Defense requested a sidebar with the Judge and presented their motion. They argued that the People failed to provide evidence that Lester's harassment was either repetitive or serious enough to be considered a 'credible threat' by a reasonable person. This was a necessary element to secure a stalking conviction. The Defense also argued that Joan did not suffer emotional distress, but that she embellished and exaggerated the impact that Lester's conduct had on her and her family. As offensive as this suggestion is, it is a Defense attorney's job to make those types of arguments. But, the Judge denied the motion and Lester's Defense began their case.

They wasted no time in leveling a number of allegations at Joan and her family. The center of their argument would be that Joan and every other witness had lied. In his opening remarks to the jury, it was clear that he was going to turn the case into a game of 'he said, she said':

Now, you're going to hear a little different version of the facts over the next half a day. You're going to learn that Lester Worthington, the Defendant in this particular case—there was a much more substantial relationship between Joan and Lester than was led on by Mrs. Eigner in this particular case. You'll learn that Lester had been over to her house numerous times at her invitation. He was close with Joe. They had played football. They had taken Joe surfing. He had played ball with Jackie, the young lady in the particular case.

You're going to learn that there was a substantial more relationship than was testified on direct. You're going to learn that Lester and Joan had an affair and it lasted for about six months... You'll learn that after that, through the last—next six or seven years they constantly talked to each other. They talked to each other on the phone. She would call him, he would call her. They conversed for a substantial time up until about 1988. She had marital problems during this period of time and to distance herself from Lester Worthington she had to make the distance greater. So she would fabricate certain things to make herself look good in, let's say, her husband's eyes.

You'll learn that the incident that was described in 1988, that Lester was invited over to her home. This took place—they got into an argument at her home. He left and then she called the police. Several witnesses will testify to the fact that Lester admitted having an affair with Joan at or about the time. You'll learn that these two neighbors, after that period, became openly hostile to each other. Both sides applied for a temporary restraining order. Both sides sued each other in the neighborhood.

You will learn that most of the alleged harassment occurred before February of 1993, yet there were few reports of this alleged outrageous conduct that took place. There were no Temporary Restraining Orders of this alleged outrageous conduct you will find from '88 through '93. You will learn that she was told that the police would do nothing because she didn't have a restraining order. She didn't even go and get one. You'll learn that there was some hostile exchange of words, but not as described by Joan in this particular case.

'You will learn that Mr. Worthington was being harassed by the Eigners to the same extent. Joe's remarks and threats to 'get' Lester. Lester's brake lines were cut. His tires were slashed. He was threatened by Joe and John. Joan called regularly.

You will learn that Lester was riding his bicycle away from his home and Mrs. Eigner came around with a camera taking pictures and almost hit him and ran him off the road. You will learn about a BB gun incident where the Eigners had shot at his house.

You will learn that the fear that was testified to in this particular case of Mrs. Eigner was not reasonable. It was exaggerated. You will learn that Lester doesn't even have a gun. You will learn that from his own family.

The testimony on the above points, coupled with some character evidence regarding what type of person Lester is, will point to a verdict of not guilty. Thank you.

When Lester was called to the stand, he repeatedly stated that he had never followed, harassed, stalked, threatened or made sexual gestures towards any member of the Eigner family. According to Lester, Joan's testimony was 'Well coached. Never happened.' He even claimed that it was in fact Joan, Akira and their children who were harassing him.

Lester accused Joan of following him and trying to run him over with her car. He accused Joe of being a drug dealer and a 'skinhead': a rather bizarre allegation given that Joe was half Japanese. He claimed Joe repeatedly vandalized both his home and car. He stated that Joe repeatedly threatened him and even shot and killed a wild bird while Lester was feeding it. He accused Akira of photographing and videotaping him, although Lester was actually in jail on the day he claimed this occurred. Lester claimed that he held a first degree black sash in Chang Ky Shing martial arts, but later admitted he had made this up in order to scare the Eigners and Detective Bradley.

Throughout his testimony, Lester displayed an open animosity towards Detective Bradley. He made inappropriate remarks that earned him several warnings from the Judge. He accused Detective Bradley of 'blackballing' him and sabotaging his efforts to obtain a restraining order against Joan. He would also go on to claim that Joan and Detective Bradley were having an affair.

Lester's most amusing and creative testimony included his description of the sexual relationship he allegedly shared with Joan in 1985, his alleged friendship with Joe and Jackie and his explanation of the events on the night he nearly ran Jackie and Melanie over.

While Lester provided contradictory evidence of the exact dates of his supposed affair with Joan, he was quite clear about the intricacies of their romantic liaisons. According to him, they started a passionate affair sometime in 1985. He claimed that it lasted approximately six to eight months, ending in about December 1985. He claimed that Joan stopped the affair because she feared Akira would find out.

Lester believed that Joan was his 'first love' and that she had taught him how to make love. He described for the court how he would come to her house every day at eleven thirty for their sexual dalliances because this is when she put the 'kids' to sleep, claiming she ran a childcare business from home. While this may have been Lester's reality, Joan has never operated a childcare business from home.

Lester claimed that he was devastated when Joan ended their affair. However, he said he understood her apprehension and fear of Akira finding out. He stated that their once close relationship then became nonexistent and that they wouldn't have any contact for two years until the day of his attempted break-in on March 1, 1988.

He testified that Joan rang him 'out of the blue' that day and asked him to come over. He explained:

> I went over to hers, jumped through the fence, went through the back yard, jumped the fence, went through the back door just like I always did, got into an argument about how to stop me and the husband from getting into this jazz we were having because he had suspicions of me. Subsequently she ended up slapping me. I slapped her back and I left. She hit me first. I slapped her. I only slapped her back.

Lester went on to testify that Joan then rang the Sheriff's Department and made a false complaint about him breaking into her home only because she was so upset by his rebuff. But Lester had provided Detective Bradley an entirely different explanation during his record of interview some five years earlier. During that interview he claimed that he was drunk at the time and had only climbed into the Eigners' backyard to let the dog out because she was barking. It would seem that Lester had been caught out lying on the stand.

When Lester was asked why he was now changing his story, he claimed that he had originally lied to Detective Bradley to prevent Akira from finding out about his affair with Joan. When asked about the tensions that existed between himself and Akira around 1988, he stated that they would regularly exchange verbal insults. He claimed that Akira called him a 'Nazi bastard' and that he called Akira things like 'pussy' and 'rice-ball' in exchange.

Lester would go on to paint himself as a model neighbor. He claimed that prior to 1988, he played baseball or football with both Joe and Jackie in the street and had even taught Joe how to surf and ride a skateboard. While both Joe and Jackie can remember Lester joining in several neighborhood football games when they were quite young, they never spent time with him alone.

As for the night he nearly ran Jackie and Melanie over, Lester provided a completely different version of events to every other witness. He testified that he had been at home that night and had decided to go to the 7-Eleven store which was located next to the taco shop where the girls went for dinner. He claimed that he hadn't seen the girls previously that evening and had no idea that they were also there. He stated he was approaching the intersection and had just shifted his truck into third gear when he noticed a speeding red vehicle heading right toward him. He claims that he was then forced to make a sharp and immediate turn at the traffic light to avoid a head-on collision, narrowly missing the girls with his truck.

Lester testified that he didn't immediately recognize who the girls were. He said that it wasn't until he made a U-turn and returned to the intersection that he realized it was Jackie and her friend. He denied taunting them and stated that he had actually returned out of concern because he saw one of the girls trip and hurt herself. He stated that the girls were hiding in some bushes as he waited at the traffic light and then Jackie started flipping him off, called him an asshole and said she was going to sue him. Lester said that he shrugged these comments off, continued to the 7-Eleven store and returned home several minutes later.

Again, this version of events was markedly different to the one he gave to Detective Bradley. During that interview, he had stated that, while he couldn't remember his whereabouts on the night, he was never near the intersection in question. He also never mentioned a near collision with another car. When asked by the Prosecutor why he didn't mention the car during his interview, Lester stated that Detective Bradley didn't ask him about the car.

Lester testified that shortly after returning home that night, Joe, John and two other 'skin-head' friends began teasing him. He stated that he was outnumbered four to one so he went into the house, grabbed a knife and snuck onto his balcony to 'keep an eye on them'. He claimed that the boys were messing around with his car, so he eventually crawled into the bushes in his front yard and hid until he was pulled out by the Deputy Sheriff.

The Defense then called Lester's mother to the stand. Gloria's testimony was similar to Lester's. She claimed that Lester had never harassed, threatened or followed Joan, and that Joan had been lying to the authorities for the past several years. She testified that about one year prior to the trial, Joan began to regularly follow Lester. Gloria denied Lester tried to run Jackie over. In fact, despite living next door to her for fifteen years, she couldn't even remember Jackie's name. However, she did testify that Lester and 'the young lady next door' had become very friendly about a year prior to that night. She claimed that Jackie used the pet name 'Les' for Lester, and that she and her friends would regularly call out to him as they walked by. About the only thing that Gloria would concede was Lester's aggressive behavior towards Joe, however, she would argue this was only due to an ongoing dispute between the two. While she could offer no evidence of it, she would accuse Joe of cutting the brake lines on Lester's car, and of throwing rocks and shooting pellets at her home.

By the time that she was done testifying, the prosecution had objected to a number of inappropriate hearsay remarks made by Gloria. This means that Gloria had made a number of baseless comments told to her by others, but to which she had no personal knowledge. The Judge agreed, and warned the Defense from allowing it to happen again.

Lester's older brother then took the stand, Along with Lester, he lived with Gloria off and on since she moved into the home in 1979. Like his mother, he admitted that he didn't know the Eigner family well. But he would provide an altogether fascinating testimony, riddled with stories that would later boggle and bemuse the Eigners. This included claims that, since 1992, Joe had threatened and taunted Lester on so many occasions that he had lost count. He also alleged that Joe threatened to shoot and kill him and Lester, and that Joan had secretly videotaped the entire scene.

Lester's older brother also said that Joan engaged in repeated acts of seduction towards both he and Lester. He claimed that from well before 1988, and up until 1993, Joan would regularly wash her car in a bikini and 'strike' poses for them because she knew they were watching. When asked to quantify the number of times this occurred, he replied, 'Two times a month. Three times a month. All the time.' When the Prosecutor asked him to describe what he meant by 'striking a pose', he replied, 'Well, if you've ever seen like the swim suit editions of SI—*Sports Illustrated*—you see women striking suggestive poses and lifting their legs when it's not necessary and just displaying her charms, if you will.'

The Defense would then call four witnesses to provide good character references for Lester. The Defense had each witness state why they believed Lester was a 'truthful' and 'peaceful' individual. Lester's best friend since high school testified about the closeness of their friendship and how they had regularly surfed, skied and gone on holidays together since they were teenagers. He stated that Lester was so honest and peaceful that he trusted his life with him. The witness was then asked if his opinion would change if he knew that in 1990 Lester had threatened to kill two state park rangers after they cited him for having his dog unleashed. The witness simply replied, 'no' and explained how he regularly let Lester babysit his five year old son.

On the stand, the ex-wife of the above witness reiterated Lester's charming qualities. She suggested he was like a 'marriage counselor' for her during her failing relationship with her husband. She testified that Lester was the most honest person she knew and that she had regularly let him babysit her son from the time he was born. She stated that she could not imagine him threatening or lying to anyone, including to police. She further stated that while she knew that Lester had assaulted his mother and older brother in May 1990, it didn't change her opinion of him as a non-violent person, and she found it very hard to believe that Lester would have threatened state park rangers. She admitted that, like Lester, she too had been in many fights with her own sister that resulted in physical injury, but it didn't mean that she was a violent person.

The mother of the first defense witness also shared with the court much of the same insights into Lester's demeanor. In her opinion, he was polite, truthful and peaceful. Like the others, she found it hard to believe that Lester would assault his family members or threaten to kill park rangers, but stated that it didn't change her opinion of him. The testimony of Lester's co-worker was no different. During their time working together, he found Lester to be an honest and non-violent individual.

The Defense then rested their case.

THE VERDICT

After hours of deliberation, the jury would deliver a crushing blow. They were hung eleven votes to one. One sole juror had prevented the unanimous decision required in US courts to secure a guilty verdict. The Judge declared a mistrial and ordered a retrial to commence within months. The Eigner family had gone through that entire ordeal for nothing.

When Joan received the phone call, she had to maintain a face of calm for ten year old Juliann. She listened to the Deputy District Attorney's explanations and apologies and quietly hung up the phone. No longer able to subdue her emotions, she collapsed onto the couch and began to sob. The years of pain, terror and helplessness that she had masterfully suppressed now engulfed her, and any shred of resolve evaporated as she felt Juliann's small arms around her. She didn't want her little girl to leave her side, but the guilt she felt was as powerful as her pain, knowing no child should have to comfort their mother in this way.

While Joan felt herself spiraling, Lester became a free man.

A CONFUSING CONVICTION

One of the first things Lester did after the mistrial was fire his Defense attorneys, claiming he could no longer afford to retain them. He then successfully requested the court to reappoint them as his counsel, meaning that the Californian tax payers would now foot the bill for Lester's legal representation at his retrial. Jury selection for the retrial started two months later on January 18, 1995, and would conclude the following day.

Just as they were being sworn in, Lester's attorneys indicated his desire to enter a plea bargain—or a negotiated guilty plea. Rather than proceed with another lengthy trial, Lester was agreeing to plead guilty to one count of Stalking and one count of Disobeying a Court Order. In return, the Prosecution agreed to drop separate counts of Stalking and Disobeying a Court Order, as well as the charge of Assault Occasioning Bodily Harm.

Days later, Lester fired his attorneys again. He claimed that they had a conflict of interest and he sought to withdraw his guilty plea. He would continue to hire, fire and rehire his attorneys for unexplained reasons. There were several hearings regarding his motion to withdraw his guilty plea and the matter would go all the way to the Court of Appeal. A final decision was ultimately reached some eighteen months later.

Lester's arguments for withdrawing his guilty plea were numerous. He claimed to be under the influence of drugs (thorazine) at the time that he entered his plea; that he had ineffective legal counsel; that his due process rights had been denied; that he had been threatened by Detective Bradley to enter the plea; that he feared for his life while in jail and he believed the plea would be his only way out; and, lastly, he claimed that he thought he was pleading guilty to assault, not stalking.

On this occasion, Joan would win a small victory. The Court of Appeal Judges found that Lester's desire to withdraw his plea had nothing to do with any of these things, but rather Lester's displeasure over the sentence that he received. In July 1996, the Court of Appeal found Lester's claims for withdrawing his guilty plea to be untruthful. A Judge in the court stated:

> I'm satisfied that the defendant was in full possession of all his faculties at the time his plea was taken; the defendant was aware as to what he was pleading to; that even if he did tell counsel that he was taking thorazine, I'm not satisfied that the defendant is telling the truth in that regard; and that it was all and has continued to be an attempt by the defendant to withdraw his plea of guilty because he doesn't like the sentence. He doesn't like the bargain that he's gotten.

Lester also realized too late that he had undermined his defense in the civil lawsuits. By pleading guilty to stalking Joan, his chances at a successful outcome in his counter civil lawsuit against her for harassment were unlikely. He would later admit that it was this issue that became the source of his 'conflict of interest' with his attorneys, as they continually advised him not to divulge this as a reason for withdrawing his plea. But Lester thought he knew best and he would write these details in a letter to the Judge only weeks after entering his plea.

Lester was sentenced to serve exactly one year in jail. This was part of his original guilty plea to one count of Stalking and one count of Disobeying a Court Order. By the time the sentence was handed down, he had already served two hundred and ninety five days in jail, which meant he only had another seventy days to serve. He was ordered to pay seven hundred and fifty dollars restitution and was placed on five years probation. Upon release, only a court restraining order—a formality for which he had a proven disrespect—would prevent him from coming back into Joan's life.

Even today, Lester would probably still contend that the turning point for him was the demise of his sexual and love affair with Joan. While he has never asserted this to Joan directly, as they have never even had so much as a conversation, he would tell the same story under oath during his evidence at trial, to the court appointed psychologist, parole and probation officers, police, 911 operators, his legal counsel, and likely anyone else that would listen.

On February 17, 1994, during an interview with the San Diego County Probation Department (to prepare a sentencing report for his conviction of stalking Joan), Lester produced a handwritten statement that included the following:

> I followed around a woman, who I loved and taught me how to make love for the first time! She was my first. Then she broke off our affair. To save her marriage but I was still in love with Joan and jellouse [sic] of her marriage. And of other men she might be seeing? So I tried to get evidence against her, so she would become mine. All I did was keep an eye on her and my only mistake was to fall in love with my first and to follow her that's all! I pray that Joan forgives me, and also that God forgives us both for what we have done and said to each other. I believe the court should grant me probation because I have truly seen the faults that I have done! And now its truly over between us. All I need is just one chance to prove myself and I promise I truly promise that I won't disappoint you plus I hope to leave the state and go to Kansas this can be verified end of my problem my leaving. I pray of you just one chance!

Lester would be given more than just *one* chance, and time and time again, he would fail to reform. In total, Joan would end up in court seven times to defend herself against his continued and clearly unrelenting abuse.

While Lester did spend some time interstate after his release from jail, it isn't clear whether he moved in a bid at reformation. In fact, it isn't clear whether he did anything to abate his need to control and harm her. One thing is very clear: Lester truly believes he and Joan were romantically and sexually involved. He quite clearly believes in the fantasy that he has created. His reality is nothing more than a sea of concocted fabrications. Of all the unbelievable things Lester would say and do, this alone has been one of the most difficult for Joan to reconcile.

HE'S BACK

While Lester served the remainder of his sentence, Joan and Akira decided with great sadness that they should sell their family home and part ways. Deep down, both probably knew that their marriage was never going to last forever, but the stress and strain of Lester's continued harassment, and the emotional toll it took on Joan, had become untenable. Akira moved to a unit in the city, they placed the home on the market, and filed for divorce.

As if that wasn't enough, Lester would continue to haunt her even from his prison cell. When the realtor came to value their home, he told her that she was legally obliged to disclose Lester's harassment and the recent court matter. She knew this would deter most buyers and likely decrease the value of her home, but she had no choice. After many frustrating months, the house eventually sold. Despite making very little profit, Joan was relieved and excited to move on. But she just couldn't catch a break.

On the day of settlement, she came home to find the section of fencing that bordered the Worthington's property chopped down. Fearing it would delay the sale, she rushed out and bought timber palings and Joe quickly rebuilt the fence with the help of two friends. Joan reported the matter to the Sheriff's Department, but decided not to make a formal complaint. When the Deputy Sheriff spoke to Lester's mother, she admitted to chopping it down but claimed it was her right as she built it in the first place. Joan simply didn't have the energy for a fight.

During the last weeks of June 1996, Jackie graduated high school and Joan and the kids moved from Via Francis Street. The family had lived there for eighteen years. They packed their belongings, the kids carved their initials in inconspicuous places, and they left. At one stage, while she was packing up the kitchen, Joan pulled out her collection of paperwork relating to Lester that had accumulated over the past eight years. Police reports, restraining orders, witness statements, court documents, hearing transcripts, and many other documents. She stared at it for a long time and believing it was all behind her, she threw everything away. It was an immensely cathartic moment for her.

PHONE CALL FROM PROBATION OFFICER 1998

Joan set about rebuilding her life. She began to allow herself the freedom to feel at ease in her own home, and the constant fear of being followed was starting to wane. But this relative sense of security was jolted by a phone call two years later, in 1998. Lester's probation officer told Joan that she was calling because she had grave concerns for Joan's safety. She said that Lester had recently tried to purchase a gun and had been discussing his plans to hurt Joan and her family. Finally, she reiterated the depths of Lester's hatred and his desperate desire for revenge.

Joan thanked the officer for calling and hung up the phone. She had absolutely no idea what she was meant to do. Sadie, her beloved guard dog, was no longer there to protect her, having died in a horrible and unexpected accident two years earlier—a day that Joan still describes as one of the worst days of her life. She hoped that because she had moved, Lester wouldn't be able to find her. It was a different world back then, when stalkers didn't have multiple search engines and social media at their fingertips to relocate their victims.

JOAN MEETS MARK 2000

Two more years passed and Joan felt as if she was truly moving on. She was still driving school buses for the LMSV School District and she kept herself busy with work, friends, church and looking after Juliann who was now a teenager. She dabbled in dating, but struggled to trust the men that came into her life—no doubt a product of her victimization. Until, when she wasn't expecting it, she met Mark.

Mark was one year her junior and a fellow member at her church. Their pastor, a long-time confidant and friend to both, excitedly introduced them to each other—knowing their shared interests and personalities were likely to make a good match.

Mark was the first of three boys born to loving parents. He grew up in San Diego and spent his childhood holidays exploring Mexican deserts, North American mountain ranges and hundreds of square miles of the Pacific Ocean with his father and two younger brothers. Hunting, fishing, surfing and hiking was second nature to him now. In 1976, he graduated from Valhalla High School and married his high school sweetheart shortly after. They had three sons together and remained married for over two decades but eventually divorced several years before he met Joan.

Joan was not enthusiastic about being set-up, but she could not deny that Mark possessed a clichéd rugged handsomeness and thirst for adventure that threatened to steal her heart. She subsequently treated his affections with caution and reservation, but eventually agreed to go hiking. Making sure she didn't give him the wrong impression, she purposefully wore the most unflattering outfit she could find—paint-stained denim overalls and an old pair of men's hiking boots. To this day, Mark still laughs when he recounts the outfit that his future wife was wearing on their first 'date'.

It didn't take him long to charm his way into her heart and Mark proposed to Joan six months later. Despite her love for Mark, the scars born by Lester were still fresh, and Joan worried he would one day return. Before she could agree to marry Mark, she warned him, 'You should probably know something about my past'. With a sense of fear and uncertainty, she told him everything about Lester and his history of obsession with her. She described her fear that he may one day show up again and impact their relationship. But Mark responded with support and compassion, and promised to protect her, whatever happened. They were married soon after.

Life was good and Lester seemed to be a part of her past. Joan still harbored dark and hidden fears about her experiences, but she honestly believed that the ordeal was at an end and that Lester was out of her life for good.

IT STARTS ALL OVER AGAIN

In late 2006, early 2007, Lester came back. By now, Joan's kids had all grown up and were living their own lives. Joe was busy working, Jackie had moved to Australia and Juliann was finishing her nursing degree. Joan was still driving buses for the LMSV School District and she and Mark were very much settled into their new life together. They had two labrador retrievers—Sammy and Beau—and spent all of their free time on a boat or trekking in the bush.

It had been nine long years since Joan had seen Lester, but he had changed very little. Ironically, his reappearance in her life coincided with a three-week trip that Jackie had taken to San Diego from Australia. Jackie was staying with Joan and Mark, and when Joan returned home from work she said to her, 'Jackie, this is the weirdest thing, I thought I was losing my mind but I saw Lester by my work today.'

And just like that, it started all over again. With all his cunning and criminal sophistication, Lester resumed where he had left off nine years prior. The first time she saw him, she was driving to work and he was standing near the bus yard staring intently at each passing bus.

The very next day, he was there again. This time, she locked eyes with him and she knew for certain that he was back. Lester too now knew he had found her. Joan immediately informed her supervisor that Lester had returned and demanded that her bus route be changed.

Joan drove her new route without incident in the weeks that followed. The school district shut down for the winter break, but Joan wasn't feeling very festive that Christmas. She knew a simple route change would not be enough to elude Lester. She knew it was only a matter of time before the game of cat and mouse would begin. But what he managed to do next exceeded even her own worst expectations.

Within days of returning from break, Joan was sitting in her parked bus when one of the school district garden trucks pulled in front of her. She glanced at the driver and her breath caught in her throat. It was him. She stared longer, but could still not register what she was seeing. It couldn't be him, she thought. Why on earth would Lester be driving a garden truck for the very same school district that employed her? She continued staring and he drove away. Joan was sure that she must have imagined it. There was simply no way a convicted stalker could be employed by the same employer as the victim, not with the mandatory criminal history and fit-and-proper-persons checks. But the very next day, she saw him again, refueling the gardening truck at the school district gas pump.

Joan was angry and confused. She went straight to the gardening shed to demand answers, but no one was there. Then she saw it. Printed neatly across the page of the employee sign in sheet was the name 'Lester Worthington'. Her blood ran cold. She stood frozen in fear and fury before finally racing straight to her supervisor's office. She demanded to know why Lester was working with them. She told her supervisor that Lester had been stalking her for years, had even gone to prison for it. Her supervisor was likewise shocked and contacted the Assistant Superintendent of Human Resources for the LMSV School District.

The Assistant Superintendent of Human Resources agreed to meet with Joan the following day and Joan told her the unbelievable history of Lester's harassment. Joan demanded to know how a convicted stalker could obtain a job that provided him access not only to children, but to the victim of his crimes as well. The Assistant Superintendent explained that Lester had been hired on a temporary basis on January 2, 2007. She admitted knowing about Lester's criminal history and his stint in prison for stalking, but she stated that she never thought his victim was someone who worked for the school district. Sadly, they never bothered to check.

The Assistant Superintendent for Human Resources told Joan that during the job interview, Lester said he wanted to get his life back on track. He said he was a hard worker and that he needed to make a fresh start. It seems that Lester was truthful on at least one of these points: the job would most definitely give him a fresh start on stalking Joan again. Indeed, only nine days after he started his job, Lester was caught looking through the employee directory by a district employee. When he asked what Lester was doing, Lester replied, 'Oh, I am looking for an old friend to see if she still works here.'

When the Assistant Superintendent finished speaking, Joan told her that she could no longer drive school buses while he was there. She said that her anxiety was crippling, and that Lester posed a real threat to her and the children she was driving. Lester was fired the next day.

Lucky for Joan, Lester didn't know her new married name and couldn't find her unlisted phone number. But that didn't stop his harassment. Throughout the rest of 2007, he engaged in conduct that could be classified more as annoying than threatening. He was regularly seen lurking around the bus yard and watching Joan. By now, most of her co-workers were aware of his past and his continued obsession of Joan, and they feared for her safety. Several even made it a point to escort her to and from her car.

While she hated living like a prisoner, she was surviving. She had the support of her work colleagues and Lester's harassment didn't seem to extend beyond his appearances in and around the bus yard. She was careful to alter her driving routes to and from work and was confident that Lester had not yet figured out where she lived. Mark was an incredible support for Joan, reacting to Lester's antics with increasing anger. He installed a security system on their property, forced Joan to purchase a handgun and enrolled her in shooting lessons. A longtime hunter, Mark was no stranger to guns and ensured they would both be ready to defend themselves should Lester come looking for them. As far as they knew, he never did.

But with Lester, things are never what they seem. While they wouldn't find out until much later, Lester did come to their home. He would drive a friend to the top of their long driveway and discuss the revenge he was plotting against her. He would draw a smiley face in green ink on her mailbox—a symbol that he later described as his criminal signature—and he eventually tried to hire someone to kill her.

ANOTHER TRIAL

The harassment continued in much the same vein throughout 2008. Lester would show up, then he would go away. Days would pass, and then he would pop up again. There was no set schedule to his obsession, but it was routine enough that Joan had come to expect it. Sometimes he was driving, sometimes he was standing, sometimes he blew her kisses, sometimes he pretended to shoot her. She was always on edge as she neared work, but most particularly when children were in her care. In one of the most litigious states in the world, Joan knew she was a major liability to the school district.

By the end of that year, Joan's patience was finally spent. She had tried to ignore and diminish the impact Lester's harassment was having on her. She wanted to show her gratitude to work for their support the previous year when they so swiftly fired him, so she kept silent and put on a brave face. But inside she was crumbling and knew she couldn't do it any longer. She wrote a letter to work and expressed her intention to take extended leave unless they could relocate her and address Lester's conduct.

JOAN GETS A RESTRAINING ORDER 2008

With the help of the school district, Joan obtained a restraining order against Lester in November 2008. The LMSV School District filed a Petition for Injunction Prohibiting Workplace Violence against Employees and the court issued a temporary restraining order. The order restricted Lester from the District Operations Centre and the bus yard, and ordered him to stay away from Joan. On November 25, 2008, Lester was served with the temporary restraining order. When the Deputy Sheriff attended Lester's house to serve it on him, Lester's mother told the officer that Lester didn't live at the residence, despite the officer having regularly seen Lester at the house.

Lester responded to the restraining order by unleashing a furious litany of lies. He immediately went to the Lemon Grove Sherriff's Department and called 911 from the lobby. He told the operator that Joan was his ex-girlfriend and that she had just driven her school bus past his house and told him he was going to prison. When the officer on the desk refused to help him, he accused him of protecting Joan because 'she was married to a police officer'. Neither claims were true.

The following week, Lester again called 911. He told the operator that Joan had just driven past his house, pointed a nine millimeter handgun at him and said, 'Next time I am going to kill you.' He again claimed that Joan was his ex-girlfriend and provided the last four digits of her vehicle's license plate number. An officer was dispatched and went to Lester's house to investigate. When the officer said that he didn't believe him, Lester took a photo of the Deputy Sheriff and yelled, 'You tell that fucking bitch to stop bothering me!'

On December 12, 2008, Lester filed for a restraining order against Joan in the San Diego Superior Court. A supporting declaration filed by his attorney accused her of harassing Lester and causing him to get fired from his job at the LMSV School District. His application was denied. Five days later, the very same court issued a permanent three year restraining order against Lester. It explicitly prohibited him from following or stalking any LMSV School District employee to or from their place of work and from following or stalking any bus.

LESTER COMES BACK 2009

For three months, Lester laid low and abided by the conditions of the restraining order. But by the following March, he could no longer suppress his needs. The first time he resurfaced, Joan saw him sitting on the side of the road as she drove to work, glaring at her as she passed. She reported the incident to her supervisor as soon as she arrived at work.

Later that day, she was driving her bus on a multi-lane freeway when she noticed a man standing under an overpass. The person was wearing camouflage pants and their car was nowhere in sight. As she neared him, she realized it was Lester. Travelling at fifty five miles an hour, she steadied her grip and tried not to panic. As she passed, he blew her a kiss. Joan returned to work and again reported the incident to her supervisor.

THE TRIAL 2009

The following morning, Lester went to the LMSV School District Operations Centre where he was spotted by two employees. Knowing Lester was breaching his restraining order, one of them said, 'Lester, you are not supposed to be here.' Lester just stared at him before turning and walking away. The employees contacted the Sheriff's Department to report the breach and a Deputy Sheriff drove to Lester's house. Lester walked out of the house before the officer reached the front door and the two spoke on the driveway.

The officer asked him why he was at the operations yard that morning, which Lester denied, stating 'I didn't go near there. I went to the café to get my newspaper, but I didn't go near the yard.' The officer reminded Lester of the conditions of the restraining order and left.

Within approximately one hour, the officer received a radio call from dispatch instructing him to contact Joan. So he did. When she finished regaling him with the twenty one year history of Lester's harassment, he and another officer immediately returned to Lester's house. When they arrived,

Lester was getting out of his car. They placed him under arrest for stalking despite his pleas that he had done nothing wrong.

During the interview at the station, the officer asked Lester if he was developmentally disabled—a standard question on the Holding Cell Checklist—to which Lester replied that he had lost fifty-six IQ points from separate brain injuries. When the officer asked him where he worked, Lester became abrasive and said, 'Oh no! I'm not going to tell you where I'm employed so you guys can come and arrest me again like that one officer who was sleeping with her did to me!'

Lester suddenly demanded to see his attorney. The interview ceased and he was charged with Stalking and Disobeying a Court Order and remanded in custody.

While Joan felt she had made a small victory, she knew that jail time would just spur him on further. She remembered her previous experience giving evidence at trial and dreaded what was to come. She had little faith that the justice system could right any of the wrongs that she had thus far endured. She would be right.

Prior to the matter being heard, the trial Judge ruled that all evidence of Lester's previous harassment of Joan was inadmissible. This meant that the jury would only hear evidence of the two incidents relevant to the current charges from March that year. It hardly painted an accurate picture of the calculated stalker that he was and provided nowhere near enough information for the jury to understand why she was in serious fear whenever she saw him. Yet, the Judge believed that any prior evidence would be too prejudicial against Lester. It was a massive blow to the prosecution, but Joan was not surprised.

Once again, she felt let down by the system that was meant to protect her. As she gave evidence and spoke about the debilitating anxiety and fear he caused her, she watched the jurors' faces betray their disbelief. Their silent mockery was as torturous as Lester's crimes. She felt belittled, ashamed and wanted off the stand.

It came as no surprise to Joan that the jury found him not guilty of the stalking charge and only convicted him for violating his restraining order. He was sentenced to jail, but was soon released.

LESTER TARGETS THE LMSV SCHOOL DISTRICT

After the trial, the permanent restraining order was still in effect, and Lester was quiet for awhile. Joan continued to drive buses and spent her days wondering when he would show up again. She knew he was still living with his mother in a home only one and a half miles from the bus yard and ensured her route was nowhere near it. For nearly eighteen months, things went incredibly quiet once more. Over that time, he would only be spotted a few times.

The last that Joan had seen or heard from Lester was at trial in July 2009. Unbeknownst to her, this was only due to his obsession with a new victim, Darren, rather than a waning interest in her. But, as he always did, he came back for her. By now she was very used to operating in a constant state of suppressed panic whenever Lester was out of jail, but particularly when she drove her bus. When she considered the risk to the children in her care, she was often engulfed with fear and guilt. Nothing ever quite prepared her for the moments when he re-entered her life, no matter how many times it happened.

It was February 2010, and she hadn't long returned to work from the Christmas break. She was driving her bus at approximately nine o'clock when she approached a pedestrian crosswalk at Spring Street and the 94 East freeway entrance. As she neared, she saw a man in camouflage pants staring at her from the edge of the crosswalk. She slowed down to let him pass, but, realizing it was Lester, she accelerated through the light. As she passed, he shouted 'Fuck you!' She immediately returned to the bus yard and reported the incident to the Sheriff's Department. She refused to drive her bus again that day.

When the Deputy Sheriff investigated the complaint, they spoke to the LMSV School District Transportation Supervisor. She would tell them that several other employees, including other bus drivers, maintenance workers and landscapers, had also reported numerous incidents where Lester pretended to shoot them. All of them occurred when they were driving past his house and most happened in February 2010.

Two incidents were particularly interesting. On February 17, 2010, two Deputy Sheriffs responded to a call from Lester's neighbor. When they arrived, the neighbor expressed his dismay at the rather large signboard that Lester had erected in his yard. The sign read, 'LMSV eat shit.' Two days later, the Deputy Sheriffs were again called to Lester's house after he blocked a LMSV School District bus in the street with his car. It was clearly a busy month for Lester. However, given that he lived so near to the bus yard, there was certainly no shortage of opportunities.

Things then went incredibly quiet once more. This time, the refuge lasted nearly a year. But on December 13, 2010, he was again spotted near the LMSV School District bus yard. That afternoon, a fellow bus driver was driving her personal vehicle away from the bus yard when she saw a man sitting on the ground next to some bushes. She reported experiencing a 'creepy' feeling because a number of school children were nearby. She thought he looked extremely out of place and made sure to get a good look at him. The man saw her watching him so he stood up to leave. As he did, she saw that he was wearing camouflage pants.

Detective Wood is appointed to Joan's case

Then, in January 2011, something happened that would later prove to be a turning point for Joan. Her case was finally handed to a seasoned detective who, like Detective Bradley in 1993, took a personal and professional interest in the matter. When Joan's case hit his desk, Detective Wood had worked with the San Diego County Sheriff's Department for nearly twenty years. Detective Wood was full of ingenuity and determination. He began investigating the matter with a passion that bolstered Joan's faith in the justice system and a vigor for which she remains eternally grateful. Just like she had with Detective Bradley, Joan knew he really cared about her and wanted to restore some level of normality to her life.

Within two months, Detective Wood would manage to collect a trove of evidence, and was confident that it would seal a conviction for multiple counts of stalking, restraining order breaches and other acts of attempted violence. Many of the charges would be for acts of aggression and violence that Joan had absolutely no idea had even occurred.

Two weeks after first spotting Lester in the bus yard, a fellow bus driver saw a flyer with Lester's picture on it in the LMSV School District Operations Center. She recognized him immediately as the man she had seen in the bushes. She told her supervisor and they called Detective Wood. They showed him the exact spot where Lester was sitting that day and he measured the distance from that location to the LMSV School District bus yard. It was only one hundred and fifty feet. This was well within the one hundred yards that was prohibited by the restraining order.

One month later, Joan was driving her personal car to work. As she approached the very same intersection where Lester had verbally abused her in February 2010, a man jumped in front of her moving car. She was forced to brake abruptly and swerve to avoid hitting him, causing everything to fly off her passenger seat. When the car finished skidding, she looked up to see Lester lunging at her car, pretending to shoot at her.

Her hands shaking so badly that she could barely grip the steering wheel, she quickly drove off. And just like that, he was back in her life again. She wanted to cry, or scream, or just throw her head into the sand. She somehow managed to drive to the bus yard and report the incident to the Sheriff's Department.

When she did, she learned that a co-worker whose personal car was very similar to Joan's, had also seen Lester at the same intersection that morning. She would later testify that she twice motioned for him to cross the road, but he shook his head from side to side as if to say 'no'. As she drove off and continued past him, she realized it was Lester, whom she remembered from his brief employment with the LMSV School District and the bulletins pinned to the walls at work. Her testimony clearly showed that Lester had been waiting at the intersection for Joan.

The Sheriff's Department was quick to respond. Not long after Joan's initial call to Detective Wood that morning, he and three other officers went to Lester's house. His mother told them that Lester wasn't home so Detective Wood left his business card with her and instructed her to have Lester ring him immediately.

The following day, Lester's attorney rang Detective Wood. He told Detective Wood that Lester refuted the allegations, then accused Joan of trying to run Lester over. The attorney further stated that 'this was their story and they were sticking with it.'

Joan refused to come into work the next day. Instead, she sat at home and considered her future. She knew that she couldn't keep working at the bus yard, and certainly couldn't keep driving children around while Lester was loose. To make matters abundantly worse, she had also recently found out that a co-worker had been directed to take discreet photographs of her on duty as part of a covert compliance exercise. Joan suspected it was part of a larger plan to discredit her hard-earned reputation in order to eradicate what had clearly become a huge liability for the LMSV School

District transportation operations. One can only imagine the emotional impact this would have on a victim of stalking.

She knew she couldn't go back to work. So she called Jackie in Australia who immediately drafted the following letter for the attention of the Assistant Superintendent of Human Resources for the LMSV School District:

To whom it may concern:

The purpose of this letter is to formally advise you of recent events and their subsequent impact on my ability to continue my employment in a manner that is safe to myself, my colleagues and the children I am entrusted to transport. Considering these events, the heightened risk they pose and the effect they have had on my physical and emotional wellbeing, it would be irresponsible for me not to formally bring these matters to your attention.

As you know, I have been the victim of longstanding stalking abuse by a male individual named Lester Worthington. These crimes have been ongoing for over twenty years, which includes the duration of my employment as a bus driver with this school district. It is not necessary to detail the full chronology of these offences (they are publicly available should you require them), suffice to say a number of attacks have occurred while undertaking my employment duties, therefore directly involving the school district. In 2009, these events culminated in a current restraining order between the school district and Mr. Worthington.

I was once again involved in an attempted attack by Mr. Worthington while travelling to work. At approximately six-thirty a.m., Mr. Worthington lunged in front of my moving vehicle causing me to take emergent and evasive action so as to avoid any impact with him. Mr. Worthington then stood in front of my car, pointed something at me and motioned to shoot. I subsequently realized that Mr. Worthington was using his hands as guns and repeatedly gestured as if he was shooting me.

Despite fearing for my life, I managed to maneuver my vehicle away from Mr. Worthington and drive the remaining distance to work. I later became aware that a co-worker had seen Mr. Worthington moments before my incident loitering in the area where he confronted my car. This matter was immediately reported to police who have issued a warrant for Mr. Worthington's arrest. While some respite is provided in knowing the police are doing everything within their power to ascertain Mr. Worthington, I now live in constant fear for my safety and believe we must do everything within our power to ensure a safe workplace for not only me and my colleagues, but also the children we transport.

There is no denying the risk Mr. Worthington poses to me and my ability to safely transport children. It would be negligent not to immediately notify the parents of these children of the potential dangers enlivened by the conduct of Mr. Worthington. I understand that these circumstances may result in my reallocation to duties that do not involve driving and, in light of the totality of these circumstances, I understand that any other action would be extremely irresponsible.

I am, and have been for the last twenty years, a victim of crime; a fact which makes the recent actions of certain colleagues unconscionable. Recently I became aware that my immediate manager had been engaging in conduct that can only be described as stalking-like behavior. I am aware that I have been the target of surveillance and covert photography by my immediate managers. The history of my abuse via the conduct of Mr. Worthington is widely known to both my colleagues and employer, yet despite this I am now being subjected to further harm by the actions of my manager.

I sincerely plead for your understanding and assistance in relation to these matters. I am, and always have been a dedicated and diligent employee and it is my commitment to my work that has necessitated me writing you this letter.

Joan was placed on leave immediately. Within days, she and the HR Department agreed to place Joan into a temporary position as a teacher's aide in a school located on the other side of the District. Joan accepted the offer, as it got her off the streets and out of harm's way. She also felt it significantly minimized the risk of innocent bystanders being harmed by Lester's actions. Fortunately, the Sheriff's Department were making solid inroads with their investigation and Lester was arrested only days later. Once he was safely locked behind bars, Joan agreed to drive her bus again.

JUSTICE AT LONG LAST

On January 25, 2011, Lester's attorney brought him into the Lemon Grove Sheriff's Station. He was taken into custody by Detective Wood but refused to answer any questions. Lester's attorney advised Detective Wood that Lester would be exercising his right to silence and he would not be talking about the allegations. So Detective Wood didn't bother giving Lester a Miranda warning and didn't attempt to interview him. Instead, Lester was transported to the San Diego Central Jail and charged with one count of Stalking with Court Order in Effect and four counts of Disobeying a Court Order.

Detective Wood then contacted a Judicial Officer and secured an Emergency Protective Order against Lester to provide a measure of protection for Joan in case Lester was granted bail and released from custody. Detective Wood also contacted the Watch Commander at the San Diego Central Jail and made arrangements for Joan to be contacted immediately if Lester was to be released. Fortunately, he never was.

On February 8, 2011, an amended complaint was filed against Lester and one count of Disobeying a Court Order was dropped. The following day, a Preliminary Hearing was held in the San Diego Superior Court and Lester pleaded not guilty to these charges. After presentation of the evidence, Lester was bound over on all counts and a trial was ordered.

The trial was originally set for March 30, 2011, the day before Joan's fifty forth birthday and twenty-three years after this whole ordeal began. But before the trial started, Detective Wood found Darren.

THE BOMBSHELL

At this time, Jackie was again on vacation from Australia and was staying with Joan and Mark. She and Joan were making the most of their last day together before Jackie returned to Australia, and were about to grab lunch when Joan received a call from a San Diego Deputy District Attorney. He told her that he had fresh information regarding her case and said it was critical that she meet with him and Detective Wood to discuss it. She and Jackie forgot about lunch and drove straight to the Sherriff's station.

When they arrived, they were ushered to a conference room and the Deputy District Attorney and Detective Wood gave a grave account of Lester's activities over the previous two years. Joan knew that Lester's contacts had slowed down somewhat since the trial in 2009, but she couldn't have dreamt it was because he was too busy plotting something more heinous. It included unbelievable tales of Lester claiming to firebomb the LMSV School District bus yard, soliciting someone to burn her house and plotting an assault on her and children on her bus.

As she listened, she felt a level of vulnerability she had never before experienced. She later described that moment like she had been ripped open and thrown to a pack of wolves. She tried to speak, but couldn't. Instead, she sat wringing her hands and trying not to cry. By the time he had finished, the Deputy District Attorney had warned her at least three times: 'He is going to kill you.'

Then they asked her something peculiar. They asked if she had ever noticed 'smiley faces' anywhere near her house, work or property. She asked what they meant and they described the infamous logo used for the 'Don't worry, be happy' campaign. The logo is comprised of two dots for eyes and an upturned line for a mouth. She had no idea why they were asking but quickly remembered a small hand-painted smiley face that mysteriously appeared on her letterbox about two years prior. At the time she thought it was probably left by a deviant school kid as a joke. Detective Wood was quick to ask whether the image was still visible. She said yes and questioned why. She could tell by the look on their faces that she probably didn't want to know.

What followed was a chilling account of a man named Darren and his fall from Lester's graces. Darren was no shrinking violet, and had a serious criminal record in California. Yet even Lester's obsessions would become too much for him. What follows is an account of Darren's evidence that he provided at court in 2011.

THE PLAN

Lester and Darren met in late 2008 and quickly became friends. It didn't take long for Lester to begin regaling Darren with stories of Joan, who he described as his 'ex-girlfriend'. He continually told Darren that he hated her and wanted to kill her and her daughter Jackie. One night, after a day of fishing together, Lester took Darren to Joan's house and said, 'This is the bitch's house and I am going to burn this shit down!'

Lester continued to tell Darren about his desire to kill the Eigner women. One day, he took Darren to his house and showed him the guns that he planned to use when he did it: two .40 caliber handguns, a nine millimeter handgun, and a .38 caliber revolver. When Darren asked him when he planned to do it, Lester told him that he was waiting until his mother passed away. He said that his mother could never survive the trauma of him going back to prison for murder, should he get caught.[2] Warrants which were later executed at Lester's house confirmed that he had access to four guns.

---

2   According to public records, Gloria Worthington died in August 2015 while Lester was detained at Atascadero Forensic Hospital.

In January 2009, Lester bought a laptop computer from Fry's Electronics. He allegedly claimed that he bought it to search for information on Joan and Jackie. However, Lester had trouble using the computer and sold it to Darren. Darren made a partial payment and was in debt to Lester for the remaining amount. Lester then offered to forgive the debt if Darren set fire to Joan's house and a bus in the LMSV School District bus yard.

On January 29, 2009, Lester picked Darren up from work and said to him, 'Let's go burn some buses.' Darren wasn't quite sure how to take him, but quickly realized that Lester was serious when he smelled the gasoline in his car. Darren refused to help him for fear of being sent back to jail. He asked Lester to drive him to his girlfriend's nearby apartment instead.

A short time later, Darren received a call from Lester, who told him to look out his window. When he did, Darren saw smoke rising from the LMSV School District bus yard. Fire crews responded and extinguished the fire, but when the smoke settled one bus was completely destroyed and another damaged. The following day Lester allegedly showed Darren a copy of the *Crime Watch* section of the *San Diego Union Tribune* newspaper that detailed the fire. He told Darren, 'That's how a man gets things done.'

Within days, Lester again approached Darren with another proposition: make an attempt on Joan's life and he would waive the debt. Lester's stalking had finally reached new depths of depravity and disregard for life and the law. Darren asked Lester what he was talking about and Lester told him that he wanted him to throw a brick at Joan's school bus. Lester took Darren to a bridge that passed over a section of Highway 125, a thirteen mile stretch of freeway that runs from the Southern suburbs of San Diego to Joan's hometown of Santee.

When they arrived, Lester showed him a brick and a pair of rubber gloves that he had brought to the scene. Presumably the gloves were to be used to conceal Darren's fingerprints should the brick ever be forensically examined. Lester then told Darren that Joan drove a 'short bus'—a colloquial term often used to describe buses that are used to transport special education, mentally impaired and physically disabled persons. He told Darren that Joan would eventually drive under the bridge because it was part of her daily route and that Darren was to drop the brick on her bus when she did.

Darren asked what he should do if he didn't see Joan's bus. Content with causing any manner of harm, Lester told him to throw it on any of the LMSV School District buses in order to send a message to Joan. When Darren asked about the possibility of children being on the bus, Lester replied that he 'didn't give a fuck about the kids'. This was a new low even by Lester's own appalling standards. It is almost incomprehensible that Lester would risk the lives of a busload of children—all of whom already suffer daily from the challenges that they were born with—in an attempt to harm Joan. As a father himself, Darren told Lester that he wouldn't do it.

LESTER STALKS DARREN 2009

Darren had now rebuffed three of Lester's propositions: He refused to burn Joan's house; he refused to burn a bus; and he wouldn't throw a brick at her bus either. His frustrations piquing, Lester now turned his fury on Darren.

On February 26, 2009, Lester demanded the money that Darren owed him and challenged him to a fight. Lester said that he was 'going to kick Darren's ass' and that he was going to 'take care' of him. The next day, Lester waited for Darren in the parking lot before work. When Darren arrived, Lester pointed his hand in the shape of a gun at him and yelled, 'I'm going to shoot you mother fucker!' Darren reported what happened to his supervisor and the California Highway Patrol were called. The officers escorted Lester from the premises and made reports of the incident.

Lester resumed his harassment of Joan alone, and it took less than one month for him to be arrested for stalking her and breaching his restraining order yet again. On March 24, 2009, he was held in custody until the trial, but, having been convicted only of the restraining order breach, Lester was free by that July. It didn't take him long to pick up from where he left off with Darren.

Within days of his release, Lester started harassing and stalking Darren. Ironically, he used many of the same tactics that he had mastered against Joan and her family. Among the many things Lester did to harass and intimidate Darren was to spray-paint smiley faces in innocuous places near Darren's apartment. Detective Wood explained to Joan that Lester claimed to have adopted the smiley face as his criminal 'signature'. In criminal offending, the term 'signature' refers to the unique and integral part of an offender's behavior, and often relates to their emotional or mental motivation for committing an offence. For Lester, the smiley face ensured his victims knew he was there. Unfortunately for Lester, Joan had no idea it was his mark until two years after he left it. That didn't diminish her disgust when it was revealed he had left his mark on her private property.

On August 3, 2009, Lester parked his car outside Darren's apartment and waited for Darren to drive to work. Just as he did to Joan all those years before, Lester pulled out behind him and began tailing his car. As he raced and paced his car with Darren's, Lester yelled and pretended to shoot him. Lester then cut him off, narrowly missing Darren's car with his own and causing Darren to swerve into oncoming traffic. Darren took evasive action and avoided a head-on collision by inches.

This was too much for Darren. He knew he had to go to the police and seek their assistance. He drove straight to the La Mesa Police Station and spoke with an officer. The officer instructed him to take out a civil restraining order.

Two days later, Darren filed a San Diego Superior Court restraining order against Lester. This was just eleven days after Lester's release from jail.

Darren was genuinely afraid for his safety and knew from watching Lester's insatiable quest for Joan that he was not likely to stop coming after him. How right he would be. What was clearly bitter for Darren would become a sweet irony for Joan. Lester was sowing the seeds of his own demise. While it would still be some time to come, the prosecution authorities now had another witness that could not only speak to Lester's chilling conduct and actions, but to his inexplicable thirst to hurt Joan and her family.

JOINING FORCES

Darren cooperated with police and provided an astonishing story that not only corroborated evidence that Lester was in fact stalking Joan but spoke of his own victimization as well. Lester was rebooked for the charges relating to Darren and the trial was adjourned.

In total, Lester was charged with seven counts of criminal acts against Darren that included one count of Stalking; Assault with Force Likely to Cause Great Bodily Injury; two counts of Solicitation to Commit a Crime (one relating to Lester's arson request at Joan's house and one relating to the requested brick-drop from the bridge); and three counts of Making a Criminal Threat. Lester was arraigned and pleaded not guilty to all charges. On May 11, 2011, Jackie's thirty third birthday, a Preliminary Hearing was held in the San Diego Superior Court regarding these charges. After presentation of the evidence, Lester was bound over on all counts except for one count of Making a Criminal Threat.

Five days later, the prosecution filed a motion to join Joan's and Darren's cases for a jury trial. On June 16, 2011, the motion was granted. Lester opposed the motion, arguing that the cases should be tried separately because one case was weaker than the other. However, the Judge felt otherwise, stating that the crimes were of the same class and factually connected.

In another blow to Lester's Defense, the Judge ruled that the evidence in the two cases was to be 'cross admissible', meaning the evidence that Lester stalked Joan was admissible concerning the charges relating to Darren and vice versa. This was hugely important because the evidence would explain why Lester solicited Darren to commit crimes of assault and arson against Joan and would show Lester's acts were calculated rather than coincidental. Moreover, there was relevant and compelling testimony from the victims and witnesses in both cases. This was a major win for Joan and the prosecution and signaled the tenor of the trial that was to come.

For Joan, this changed everything. She could still hardly believe that a new witness had been found; someone who could speak of Lester's sinister plans for her and Jackie; who had likewise suffered his cruel and selfish obsessions. Despite the concern that she felt for Darren's own suffering, he was a welcome ally. As a fellow witness, they were prohibited from contact, but every day after she learned of his existence and his continued refusal to hurt her, she wanted to say thank you. She understood that, although he never came forward on his own volition to tell the police of Lester's sickening attempts on her life and property, he was stepping up now. And for Joan and her family, that was all that mattered.

Darren's story would show the world that Joan was not a liar. She was not prone to exaggeration, drama, self-interest, scorn or any of the other spurious allegations that Lester and his attorney had leveled at her so many times before. Darren was an independent person that didn't know her or her family. He certainly had no reason to lie for them and she knew the jury would see that. She wouldn't have to endure their critical, pitiless stares this time around. She knew that she would, at long last, be believed. She knew that she wouldn't be seen as the 'crazy lady' that she had been dubbed all those years before.

This time she wasn't going to be alone in trying to convince a jury that Lester was erratic, obsessive and volatile, and that, left unchecked, he would end up killing someone. This time, she knew that it was no longer just her battle, but the Sheriff's Department, the District Attorney's and Darren's as well. *Finally,* she thought, *everyone will see the magnitude of Lester's obsession, what I have had to survive and the toll it has taken on me.*

THE TRIAL 2011

On September 14, 2011, the trial commenced in the Superior Court of California in downtown San Diego. In all, Lester stood trial for a total of ten charges relating to his criminal conduct against Joan and Darren.

This was by far the largest of the three criminal trials Joan had been involved with; and for the first time ever, evidence of Lester's previous stalking and criminal offending against Joan would be admissible, as well as evidence of uncharged acts. This evidence would show Lester's long history of tormenting Joan and her family, all the way back to the beginning in 1988. It also meant that the prosecution could introduce evidence of incidents that didn't eventuate into an arrest, including the night that Lester tried to run Jackie and her friend over with his truck. This evidence would be used to show the jury that Joan wasn't exaggerating when she claimed to be in reasonable fear for her safety and that of her immediate family. This was another massive win for her and the prosecution.

In total, the prosecution submitted thirty-three witnesses that they were prepared to call. The Deputy District Attorney was going to make sure that the jury could come to no other conclusion except 'guilty'. Joan was the first witness to take the stand. She was again forced to come face to face with the man she had feared for so long and had now come to hate. But this time, she felt a calm that she had never before been able to summon. As much as she didn't want to endure the depleting experience of testifying again, this time she knew it was different. This time she looked at the jury when she spoke. She wanted them to see her as a real person: a mother, a grandmother, a wife.

When she was on the stand, she was feeling nervous, but she wasn't emotional. Despite everything that had happened, she felt very much in control. She surprised even herself. She remembers the Deputy District Attorney telling her it was okay to show more emotion.

She searched herself to find it, but she just didn't have anything left to give. Emotionally and physically, she was spent: twenty-three years of being stalked had taken its toll.

Joan testified for two days. She thought Lester's attorney was oddly subdued compared to his previous appearances and his attempts to discredit her seemed lackluster. Perhaps Lester's Attorney was feeling hamstrung, as the prosecution's case was virtually impenetrable.

As she bravely answered question after question for the jury, she couldn't help but remember the effect that her sufferance had had on her parents in previous trials. With her father now passed for nearly seven years and her mother too frail from cancer treatments to attend, she was humbled by the support and strength that Mark gave her. He was a major advocate and force in her life. He had endured the tears, the pain, and the fear with her every step of the way and was her voice of reason and resolve when she wanted to hide from her reality.

Joan was able to tell her story from the beginning: from the moment she found Lester breaking into her bedroom to the subsequent years of harassment, threats, stalking and abuse of her family. From the bizarre to the crude and the downright terrifying, she laid bare the years of abuse she had suffered: the violent outbursts, the simulated shooting, the sexually explicit remarks, the repulsive tongue wagging gestures, the following, the phone calls, the gun-waving, the peeping, the masturbating—the scars that Lester had carved into her life.

Despite her resolve, she still found it hard to look at him in court. She felt that he enjoyed seeing her discomfort and she tried very hard not to give him the satisfaction. She had testified before him enough times to come to believe that he probably lived for those days, those moments that he could be in her presence. She doubted very much that he cared about the circumstances under which their acquaintance could be made. It was almost as if court, for him, was the climax to his stalking journey. It was sickening.

To her, he appeared a lonely and pathetic figure. By now, both she and Lester were aged in their fifties. And while he didn't have any children, she was now a grandmother. *Who stalks a grandma!?* she thought. The only person who attended court to support Lester was his mother. Time had definitely taken its toll on Gloria Worthington's health. She moved herself into and out of the courtroom with great difficulty, requiring the use of a steel walking-frame. Despite her previously outspoken and derogatory behavior towards Joan and her family, she sat rather quietly and complacent. Perhaps she too could see the senselessness of Lester's pleas of innocence.

When Joan finished her testimony, the prosecution paraded witness after witness to speak of Lester's ongoing offending. Even Jackie took the stand after flying nearly eight thousand miles from Melbourne, Australia, to tell her side of the story. For her, the chance to confront Lester was more than welcomed. She recalls:

> The last time that I had seen him, I was testifying for my mom at his trial in 1994. I was only fifteen years old. Still a child in the eye of the law, I walked alone into a courtroom of strangers to face a man that I had feared for most of my life. I was far too young to understand the mechanics of the justice system or the gravity of the situation. At times, I couldn't even follow the legal jargon. This time, I was a grown woman. I was a mother, a scholar and had worked in law enforcement for over a decade. Over the years, I had studied and spoken to plenty of men just like Lester. I understood the power and pleasure he most likely felt in hurting my mom. This time, I wasn't scared. I craved a second chance to show him that we were going to fight back. That we would always fight back.
>
> I remember sitting outside the courtroom waiting for my turn to testify. My dad was there, but as a fellow witness, we really couldn't talk. My sister, Juliann, had arrived to support us and she went inside the courtroom to watch other testimony

and wait for us to take the stand. It was really comforting knowing she would be inside the courtroom with me. I was later told that Lester mistook her for me and became extremely agitated. He began calling out that I couldn't be in the courtroom because I was a witness.

I remember seeing Darren for the first time. He was waiting to testify and he looked nervous. I had an overwhelming urge to thank him for helping our family. I knew he was fighting his own battles with Lester, but I also knew that his testimony was crucial for mom's case. But, being barred from speaking to other witnesses, I said nothing. At one stage he looked at me and simply said 'sorry'.

Darren then went on to testify. He was on the stand for a while, but it wasn't hours. Juliann later described him as a great witness. While he was hardly dressed for an appearance at Superior Court—baggy jeans, oversized hooded sweatshirt and Rastafarian-colored beanie—he won the jury with his forthright answers and comical disdain for Lester's attorney. At one stage, Lester's Attorney phrased a question about the nature of their friendship. Darren thought he was suggesting the two were lovers and he was very quick to set that record straight.

Dad was next. He wasn't on the stand long. For Dad, testifying at the trial in 2011 meant that, in some small way, he could have that second chance to help my mom. It was always odd to me—and most people want to understand—why he never did more to protect my mom and his kids from Lester when they were married. Hindsight always brings much clarity, so I wasn't surprised when he once explained to me that he would do it differently if he could go back. But at the time, he was scared to act, scared to hurt Lester because he feared he would end up in jail.

Dad handled himself well on the stand that day. Lester's Attorney didn't have many questions for him, but he did ask about the day Lester pulled a gun on him and Joe.

He asked Dad whether the gun was real or fake. Dad told him that he didn't bother to ask Lester and that he was neither an expert with handguns nor blessed with eyesight capable of identifying real guns from fake ones at a distance of thirty yards. Apparently this made the jury chuckle.

It felt like Dad was out of the courtroom within minutes. I was up next. It was with a fantastic feeling of nerves and redemption that I swore to tell the truth and took my seat in the witness stand. I looked at Lester and I hardly recognized him. He no longer had the long stringy hair that I could so clearly remember. In fact, he had very little hair at all.

The Deputy District Attorney asked a few introductory questions, then we covered the night that Lester tried to run Melanie and I over. Then it was the turn of Lester's Attorney. He didn't bother standing, and he certainly didn't approach the stand to hover over me like Lester's previous attorney. To be honest, I was slightly disappointed. I was ready for a fight. I wanted a fight. I wanted him to see the anger that I have harbored for everything Lester had done to my mom. But instead, he asked me two questions. One relating to the night Lester tried to hit us with his car, the other about who paid for my plane ticket to appear in court that day. And then I was dismissed. It was over. It felt all very anticlimactic. The deflation of Lester's Attorney was clearly visible. A sign that I took to mean we were winning.

The verdict

After fourteen days of submissions and testimony, the trial was finally over. The Judge gave his final instructions to the jury and Joan was left to wait. Juries are a funny thing. For most people who serve on a jury, it will be their first time to experience the machinations of a criminal trial with all its theatre, drama, imperfections and onerous responsibilities.

And when it is all over, you never know what they will do. Having been burned several times before, Joan couldn't help but feel anxious about the verdict, no matter how much evidence was presented.

The Deputy District Attorney and Detective Wood both warned her that the jury may deliberate for many hours, even days. They tried to pacify her fear that Lester would again be set free. They also told her that it was highly unlikely that the jury would convict Lester on all ten counts. They said they would be happy if he was convicted on six. She thanked them for their honesty and started the long wait. And eventually, the call came.

Joan took the call and Jackie stood anxiously watching her. It was Detective Wood. The call didn't last long and he did most of the talking. But Joan was smiling. She thanked Detective Wood, disconnected the call and shouted, 'Guilty on nine counts! Nine counts!'

She was stunned. Even the Deputy District Attorney and Detective Wood couldn't believe their success. Lester had been found guilty on every charge except one misdemeanor count of Disobeying a Court Order. The two women danced, they hugged and yelped in wild excitement. As the shock of the moment began to wear off. Joan started crying. It had truly been the longest journey.

THE SENTENCE

Now all that was left to do was pray for a long prison sentence and wait for the sentencing hearing. But waiting was something that Joan was used to. The maximum prison sentence that could be imposed was eight years and four months. The hearing was scheduled for October 19, 2011 when the Judge would decide Lester's fate. This meant the District Attorney and San Diego County Probation Department had about two weeks to prepare and submit their recommendations for Lester's sentence. Both submissions were highly unfavorable for Lester. The Probation Officer's report concluded:

The defendant did not express any feelings of empathy for either victim, and blamed both of them for the circumstances surrounding the Instant Offense. The defendant seemed completely unaffected by his time in custody, and expressed his ongoing anger with both victims. Additionally, the defendant believed the jury only convicted him on these counts because 'it was Friday and they did not want to waste another week away from work' ... Most disturbing of all, the defendant does not seem to view any of his actions or attitudes as inappropriate, even when these ideas are challenged with more logical and socially acceptable ideas. He seems to have a deeply ingrained pattern of critical thinking, blaming others for his actions and accepting no personal responsibility.'

The Probation Officer surmised that Lester was not amenable to rehabilitation at the local level and recommended that he be removed from the community for a significant period of time. The report went on to say:

Without a significant period of custody, it seems likely the defendant is on a collision course with these victims where someone may lose a life.

The Probation Officer recommended that probation be denied and that Lester serve the maximum term of imprisonment of eight years and four months. Lester's prior convictions excluded him from consideration for local prison.

On the day of the hearing, the District Attorney and the Deputy District Attorney delivered their sentencing submission. The prosecution submission was compelling:

The People believe the Defendant is a danger to Joan W, her daughter and Darren and that his conduct is so egregious that he must be sentenced to prison for a significant period of time ... The sentencing options vary widely in this case, ranging from probation (if specific findings are made) up to eight years and four months in prison ... The People request the maximum sentence in this case.

Their critique of Lester was devastating:

> The Defendant has been stalking Joan W. for over twenty-two years in spite of numerous restraining orders forbidding him to do so and convictions have sanctioned him for doing so. He has acted with disregard to the public in his actions towards Joan W. He has inflicted emotional injury upon the victims and their families. The defendant has demonstrated criminal sophistication in his behavior towards his victims. He has used computers to track down the victims and stolen employee directories. The defendant has a pattern of violent and unpredictable behavior. His performance history on probation has been unsatisfactory. He has taken no responsibility for his actions. Lastly, and most importantly, defendant has made open threats to kill Joan W., her daughter and [Darren] ... He has made threats to drop bricks on Joan W's bus with no regard for the welfare of the special needs students that may be on the bus. He has vowed to kill Joan W and her daughter when his elderly mother dies. He has engaged in dangerous activities, which are a threat to the victims and the public. He has continually used his car as a weapon and assaulted numerous people with his car dating back to 1993. The seriousness of (the) Defendant's conviction is increasing and there are multiple victims. The Defendant's prior history on probation was unsatisfactory. Finally, the factors in mitigation are nonexistent. As a result, the People request the Defendant be sentenced to eight years four months in state prison which is consistent with the Probation Department recommendation.

In addition to the Probation Officer's report and the District Attorney's submissions, the Judge reviewed a number of victim impact statements before making his final ruling. Joan told of the agonizing journey that she had endured and the many ways it had transformed her life. But one particular statement, submitted by the Assistant Superintendent of Human Resources for the LMSV School District, articulately illustrated the unintended impacts of stalking that so commonly reach well beyond just the victim. She wrote:

> Thank you for allowing me to share the emotional, physical and financial impacts Mr. Worthington's crimes have had on the La Mesa Spring Valley School District, our valued employee Joan W., other employees, children in our district and myself.
>
> In January 2007, Joan W. entered my office visibly shaking, with fear in her eyes and frustration and anger in her voice. It was during our meeting, when she shared her shock that Mr. Worthington was working right next door to her, that I quickly understood that Joan W. was a terrified victim in every sense of the word. It was only over time that I came to realize that everyone close to Joan W. and this case are also victims of Mr. Worthington's crimes.
>
> For more than three years our District has spent thousands of dollars in legal fees to deal with Mr. Worthington and his crime against Joan W and other employees. Because he would not stay away from our property and Joan W., we had to hire attorneys and apply for a restraining order. It was necessary to provide release time for at least five employees to meet with attorneys and prepare and testify in three separate trials. At one juncture, shortly before Mr. Worthington's most recent arrest, we had to place Joan W. on an alternate assignment on a middle school campus to keep her safe and reduce her stress. This required a substitute to drive her bus routes, ultimately costing the district hundreds of dollars. In this era of extreme budget cuts, you can well imagine how spending precious dollars to keep a stalker away is not something we, as the custodian of taxpayers hard-earned money, want to do.
>
> The emotional toll of Mr. Worthington's presence in our school community has been difficult for all transportation employees as well as those who work in the maintenance department. Over the years, employees who testified at his trials have called me to share their extreme frustration that

Mr. Worthington was once again acting in a threatening manner. I was told how scary it is to be a bus driver transporting students with special needs and not feeling as if you can relax. When a driver has to constantly look over his/her shoulder in fear that a convicted stalker is going to jump out in front of your vehicle, it is very scary for the driver and very dangerous for the innocent children.

On a personal note, I am very worried for my safety in the future. Mr. Worthington has proven he is revengeful. When a convicted stalker has come to your house, damaged your property and the property of your co-workers, it is creepy to say the least. The idea of Mr. Worthington plotting his next crime against a La Mesa Spring Valley employee makes me want to throw up. I get very angry and lose sleep when I imagine Mr. Worthington having access to the students and employees in our community. In my sixteen years as an administrator in the La Mesa Spring Valley School District I have dealt with thousands of individuals and hundreds of conflicts. I conclude that Mr. Worthington is by far the most worrisome because, as characteristic of a stalker, he shows no remorse.

Over the past three years our district has tried to support Joan W., but I seriously doubt her fear, and the fear of others, will vanish quickly—it is akin to Posttraumatic Stress syndrome. Mr. Worthington has proven he can lure others to believe his lies and participate in his crime and I am extremely worried that he will not be quickly or easily rehabilitated. While Joan W. is a strong, honest, hardworking woman, there are limits to what anyone can endure. She and her family deserve a life free of fear and the district's children and employees deserve the same. I plead with you to give us peace of mind, and an end to this trauma, by sentencing Mr. Worthington to the maximum number of years allowed under the law.'

The presiding Judge ordered Lester to serve the maximum sentence. He was immediately removed from the court room and returned to jail.

When Joan received the call, she was speechless. The news was momentarily paralyzing as she began to imagine her next eight years of freedom. It would take a long while, but the sense of disbelief would finally become elation. She called the people closest to her and shared the amazing news. She called Jackie in Australia and the two reflected on the implications of the Judge's decision. This meant that Joan could stay in the home she loved and wouldn't have to start a desperate search for employment at fifty-four years of age.

For Joan and her family there was a feeling of relief and closure that the ordeal had come to an end and finally, at long last, justice had been delivered. While they all knew that Lester would again be free one day, eight years seemed like a very long time away, and the immediate future was looking very bright.

But like so many times before, the cards seemed to fall in Lester's favor.

BITTERSWEET

It came as little surprise when Lester filed his appeal against his convictions. Joan wasn't particularly concerned that he would win, but she still longed for the ruling. And it wasn't going to be a quick process. Lester claimed that the trial court had erred on four separate grounds, that the evidence presented during trial was insufficient to support his conviction for stalking Joan, and that the cumulative errors warranted reversal. In other words, he believed the Court of Appeal should reverse his conviction.

He also filed a petition for writ of *habeas corpus*, arguing that his Attorney provided ineffective representation at his trial. A writ of *habeas corpus* is a tool that can be used by an offender to challenge their conviction. '*Habeas corpus*' is a Latin phrase that means, 'that you have the body.' The 'body' in the phrase means the body of someone who is in state custody because they allegedly committed a crime. In California, the right of a prisoner to file a writ of *habeas corpus* petition is guaranteed by the California Constitution. However, the petitioner must provide a strong claim for filing.

In March 2013, seventeen months after his original conviction, the Court of Appeal denied all but one of his claims. They concluded that the imposition of the sentence should be 'stayed' on three of the original counts: two counts of disobeying a court order and one count of making a criminal threat. This decision was based in legal precedent, which dictates that when a defendant is convicted of multiple counts that are all connected to one course of conduct, the defendant can only be punished for one of those counts. Fortunately, the decision had no impact on the duration of Lester's overall sentence.

But again, the relief of this decision would be short-lived.

In late 2013, Joan received a call from the California Department of Corrections and Rehabilitation (CDCR). They informed her that Lester would be out of prison in July 2015. She couldn't make sense of what she was hearing. It hadn't been long since his appeal was almost wholly denied and she was finally starting to get through life without thinking about him every single day. And now she was learning that she truly was embracing a false sense of hope and security. July 2015 wasn't even two years away. She fired off questions and was livid to learn that this inconvenient truth was something that was never explained to her.

Although the great state of California was the first place in the world to pass laws to combat the crime of stalking, in 2009 the rights of victims and public safety were relegated behind the rights of prisoners. After a state of emergency was declared in 2006 with respect to prison overcrowding, three Federal Court Judges issued what US Supreme Court Justice Antonin Scalia has dubbed 'perhaps the most radical injunction issued by a court in our nation's history.' At its peak that year, California housed one hundred and sixty-three thousand inmates; California's prisons are designed to house a population just under eighty thousand.

On August 4, 2009, the three Judges ordered that the state of California must release upward of forty-six thousand prisoners within two years. As Justice Alito pointedly observed, that was the equivalent of three Army divisions.

This order was the culmination of two decades of nonstop litigation by prisoner advocates who argued that poor health care in Californian prisons violated the constitutional ban on cruel and unusual punishment. The Eighth Amendment of the US Constitution says, 'Excessive bail shall not be required, nor excessive fines imposed, nor cruel and unusual punishments inflicted.'

For readers outside the US, under the *Prison Litigation Reform Act* (PLRA), passed by the US Congress in 1996, a three-Judge panel can be appointed to order reductions in the prison population. The PLRA also requires that, in relation to a civil action with respect to prison conditions, 'a court must give substantial weight to any adverse impact on public safety or the operation of a criminal justice system caused by the relief.'

On September 3, 2009, the State of California appealed the order of the three-Judge panel to the US Supreme Court on the grounds that it violated the PLRA and did not take into account the impact on public safety. They further argued that it demonstrated Federal Court interference with California's prison management system. But in May 2011, in a five to four decision, the US Supreme Court affirmed the three-Judge panel's finding that overcrowding is the primary source of unconstitutional medical care, and ordered California to reduce its prison population to 137.5 per cent of design capacity (or 109,805 prisoners).

Essentially, the US Supreme Court held that prison medical and mental healthcare fell below the constitutional standard of care. But as Justice Scalia opined, this finding was a judicial travesty:

> Most of them will not be prisoners with medical conditions or severe mental illness; and many will undoubtedly be fine physical specimens who have developed intimidating muscles pumping iron in the prison gym.

Further, it would appear that the Federal Court Judges ignored the correlation between California's then increasing prison population and the sharp decline in violent crime. In other words, while the prison population in California had grown, the amount of violent crime was decreasing. If they needed any precedent in making their decision, they should have learned from the disastrous results of a similar move made in Philadelphia in the 1990's. As a result of intervention by Federal Courts, thousands of prison inmates in Philadelphia were set free, and the consequences were grave. During an eighteen month period, thousands of these prisoners were rearrested for committing over nine thousand new crimes, including seventy nine murders, ninety rapes, over one thousand assaults, more than nine hundred robberies, seven hundred burglaries, two-and-a-half thousand thefts, and thousands of drug offences.

Since 2006, the State of California has reduced its prison population by more than forty three thousand. They have spent more than one billion dollars on new healthcare facilities for prisoners, and have hundreds of new doctors, nurses and support staff. Incidentally, in an era when state government budgets have been under severe pressure, taxpayers have picked up both sides of the legal bills which, from 1997 to 2009 alone, exceeded thirty eight million dollars.

The inmate population in California is now, reportedly, under control. The state of emergency was rescinded in January 2013, and the population is sitting around one hundred and forty per cent design capacity. California's politicians have declared victory on their war on prison overcrowding.

Unfortunately, victims like Joan are left asking how a system could let them down so terrifically. The effects of which will see the criminals who have wronged and hurt them, who have consumed their life, walk free from prison years sooner than they should be. The early release scheme in California continues.

For Joan, the charade is painful to swallow. Not only did her hard earned tax dollars fund years of legal proceedings to put Lester in jail; they were also making sure he was going to receive far better access to healthcare than her or any of her family members. In a country where the public versus private healthcare debate is bitterly divided, it is a sad irony that criminals in California will have far better access to free healthcare than many law-abiding citizens.

ONE MORE BATTLE

In 2014, Joan received a letter from the CDCR. She stared at it for a long time, knowing she had to open it but not wanting to. The past three years had been serene. She came and went as she pleased, not needing to alter her routines or constantly check that she was being followed. She visited her children and grandchildren whenever she wanted, not worried that Lester would turn up. She continued driving her school bus, and with her newfound freedom she started playing golf and quilting. Life actually felt normal. But as she stared at the letter in her hand, something told her that was all about to end.

She made a pot of coffee and left the letter in the study. She knew it was going to bear bad news. When she was finally ready, she went back for the letter and opened it. There it was in black and white. Lester was going to be released sooner than expected. Confused, she rang the number listed on the letter and was told that Lester had received a good behavior bond and six months were being slashed from his sentence.

What little faith she had left in the criminal justice system evaporated in that moment, but she hardly had the energy to be upset anymore. This was her life. She accepted Lester now for what he was and what he would try to take from her until the end of his days. But the fear no longer controlled her.

It served only to strengthen a resolve that has been hardened by battle. From restraining order to restraining order, court case to court case, one dejecting defeat after another. She was certainly not ready to lie down now.

Joan first contacted Detective Wood and the Deputy District Attorney who was the prosecutor in the 2011 trial. She had a barrage of questions but essentially she wanted to know whether there was anything that could be done to stop Lester's impending release. Neither could provide her with any hopeful ideas, but they did explain some interesting developments.

Detective Wood explained that while Lester was serving time in prison, his communication was being closely monitored in order to identify any perceived threats to Joan or her family. But what the San Diego Sheriff's Department identified instead were threats to their own members as well as the Deputy District Attorney. Presumably individuals Lester now blamed for his current predicament. What this meant for Lester was that he now had the full attention of the Sheriff's Department's Threat Assessment Group, a team within the Special Investigations Division whose mandate is to protect officers against whom threats have been made. For Joan, this meant that she had a welcome ally.

Detective Wood told Joan that she needed to call a Detective working in the Threat Assessment Group, and explain who she was. Joan thanked him and called the Detective straight away. She wasn't quite sure what to expect, but she found the Detective to be engaged and emphatic in her desire to help. The Detective explained her role in protecting her colleagues from Lester and promised Joan she would do everything in her power to protect her too. Joan found her compassion truly humbling.

Joan also contacted her long-time counsel and friend, Chuck Nachand. She asked him what she could do to fight Lester's early release and sought advice about her future with the LMSV School District given that she was probably going to be considered a significant liability once Lester was out of prison. He suggested ringing his colleague, Marian Birge, Attorney at Law. He explained that Marian had a very strong record in employment law and with assisting victims of harassment and abuse.

Joan contacted Marian and explained her story. With a passion and tenacity that Joan would quickly come to understand is unique to this truly amazing woman, Marian told Joan she wanted to work her case. Furthermore, she wanted to do so *pro bono*. To this day, she has never asked Joan for money.

Meanwhile Mark started searching the Internet for any kind of organization that might be able to help. He eventually came across 'Safe at Home', an address confidentiality program administered by the California Secretary of State's office. The program is designed to help victims and survivors of domestic violence, stalking or sexual assault achieve and maintain anonymity and start new lives. Some of the services they provide include suppression of Department of Motor Vehicle records, and confidential mail forwarding, name change and voter registration.

Mark and Joan were very interested and scheduled a time to meet with one of their counselors. The counselor was incredibly kind and empathetic as he explained exactly how the program worked and what services they might offer Joan and her family. He explained that while it wasn't witness protection, she would need to close every door of her previous life so Lester had no way to trace her whereabouts.

It felt like a fairly dramatic move, but Mark and Joan knew it needed to finally happen. But just as arrangements were being made, Safe at Home notified Joan that she could not qualify for the program as long as she continued working for the LMSV School District. She briefly considered quitting her job, but for a number of reasons—most notably that she didn't want to concede defeat to Lester—she didn't.

Still eager to help, Safe at Home organized a meeting for Joan and one of their attorneys. After speaking with Joan and hearing tale after tale of Lester's years of obsession and abuse, the attorney contacted the CDCR to establish and ensure strict conditions were placed on Lester's parole order. In the end, it was decided that Lester would need to wear a permanent monitoring device, reside in Orange County (about an hour and twenty minute drive from San Diego) and couldn't come within one hundred miles of San Diego. It was welcome news, but Joan was still scared.

In the meantime Marian was reaching out to anyone she could think of. In November 2014, she wrote to the California Substance Abuse Treatment Facility at Corcoran State Prison and provided an account of Lester's criminal and personal history and urged them to reconsider his conditional release. In elegant legal prose, she set out the full extent of his harassment and crimes against Joan and her family. She questioned why, in an era of high profile school shootings and killing sprees, offenders cannot be stopped before they are able to commit their horrific crimes. For Marian, the case of Lester Worthington presented an opportunity to prevent a potential atrocity through psychiatric intervention and involuntarily treatment as a 'mentally disordered offender' (MDO).

THE MENTALLY DISORDERED OFFENDERS PROGRAM[3]

> In 1986, the California Legislature enacted the Mentally Disordered Offender (MDO) law. The intent of the MDO law is to provide mental health treatment to those suffering from severe mental health disorders prior to, during, and even after their parole. The dual purpose of this law is to protect society from certain prisoners with dangerous, treatable mental disorders; and to provide treatment for those prisoners. The law requires that a prisoner who meets the following six criteria be treated by the California Department of State Hospitals as a condition of their parole:

---

3   Please refer to http://www.dsh.ca.gov/forensics/MDO.asp for further information on the MDO program.

1. The prisoner has a severe mental disorder;

2. The prisoner used force or violence or caused serious bodily injury in one of the prisoner's commitment crimes;

3. The severe mental disorder was one of the causes of or was an aggravating factor in the commission of the crime for which the prisoner was sentenced to prison;

4. The prisoner's 'severe mental disorder is not in remission' or 'cannot be kept in remission without treatment';

5. The prisoner had been in treatment for the severe mental disorder for ninety (90) days or more within the year prior to the prisoner's parole or release; and

6. As a result of the severe mental disorder, the prisoner represents a 'substantial danger of physical harm to others'.

Inmates begin the MDO treatment program inpatient at a state hospital. For males, treatment is received at Atascadero State Hospital in San Luis Obispo, while females receive treatment at Patton State Hospital in San Bernardino. When the hospital treatment team believe a patient can be safely and effectively treated on an outpatient basis, they will recommend transfer to outpatient treatment in the Conditional Release Program.[4] The patient's parole and treatment by the Department of

---

4   Once psychiatric symptoms have been stabilized and a MDO patient is no longer considered dangerous, the state hospital medical director can recommend outpatient treatment under the Conditional Release Program. Individuals must agree to follow a treatment plan designed by the outpatient supervisor and approved by the committing court, and can be moved into community outpatient settings. The court-approved treatment plan includes provisions for involuntary outpatient services such as individual and group therapies, home visits, substance abuse screenings and psychological assessments. Evaluations and assessments are done upon entry into the community and throughout the Conditional Release Program treatment. Individuals who do not comply with treatment may be returned, upon court approval, to inpatient status.

State Hospitals will be reviewed every year. The patient may remain in the MDO treatment program, either in the hospital or in the Conditional Release Program, throughout their time on parole, depending on progress. Parolees are generally required to remain on parole for three years. However, up to one year can be added when parole violations result in parole revocations. At the end of parole, the patient may be civilly committed to further periods of treatment if the court finds that the patient's mental disorder still meets certain criteria.

Marian also reached out to California State Senator Joel Anderson.[5] Re-elected in 2014, Senator Anderson had demonstrated a strong record on law and order and the LMSV School District falls within his electorate. Together with his aide, Marian started petitioning the CDCR to re-evaluate Lester's status as a MDO before releasing him onto parole. At the persistence of these two incredible women, two separate evaluations were conducted. So Joan and her family anxiously awaited the results.

On February 6, 2015, only days before Lester was due to be released, Joan finally received an update. She was driving to meet the new Human Resources Manager to discuss taking an imminent leave of absence from

---

5   Senator Anderson was elected in 2010 to represent the citizens of San Diego and Riverside Counties in the thirty-sixth Senate district. In 2014, he was re-elected to office, representing the thirty-eighth Senate district. He is a member of the Senate Public Safety Committee, the Senate Judiciary Committee, the Senate Committee on Elections and Constitutional Amendments, and the Senate Budget and Fiscal Review Committee. His work in improving law and order in California includes joining forces with the state's sheriffs and district attorneys to curb the rampant crime of metal theft in 2008. He was later named 'Legislator of the Year' for his commitment to this project. In 2012, as Vice-Chair of the Senate Public Safety Committee, Senator Anderson authorized *Senate Bill 1371*, which closed a legal loophole that convicted criminals were exploiting to evade restitution payments to their victims.

work. She knew she couldn't drive a bus for the district with Lester out of prison. But her cell phone rang before she arrived.

She pulled her car to the side of the road and answered. It was an official from the CDCR. The MDO evaluations had been returned and Lester was deemed mentally disordered. She sat in a state of disbelief as the official went on to explain what this now meant for Lester and for Joan. In two days time, instead of being released from Corcoran prison, Lester would be transported by armed guards to the Atascadero State Hospital.

Located on the Central Coast of California, Atascadero State Hospital is an all-male, maximum-security facility for mentally ill and disordered inmates. It opened in 1954 and is currently licensed to operate one thousand two hundred and seventy-five beds. There are four primary commitment categories of patients at Atascadero, but MDO patients are the most common (fifty four per cent). The hospital has been portrayed several times in popular culture, including the blockbuster film *Terminator 2: Judgment Day*, where Sarah Connor is institutionalized at 'Pescadero State Hospital'—a mental institute heavily based on Atascadero.

It was an amazing and unexpected outcome and both women burst into tears. Joan didn't understand the extent of the details just yet, but she thanked the official from the CDCR and immediately called Mark. Overcome with his own tears of relief, together they cried at the gift of living free from Lester's terror just a bit longer. Joan then called Marian, knowing that none of this would have happened without her selfless persistence. Joan had no idea how to adequately thank her but the emotion in her voice said it all. Joan then called family and friends. For the next hour she shared the news with everyone she could think of who had loved and supported her over the past twenty-seven years.

She made her way home through an array of emotions. She felt confused but relieved, excited but apprehensive, happy but anxious. It really wasn't the outcome that she had prepared for and the stress of the preceding weeks had been intense. When she arrived home, she turned on her computer and Googled Atascadero. She had never heard of it before and grew more fascinated as she read. It seemed Lester had finally gotten what he deserved and would hopefully receive the treatment that he so badly needed.

Lester arrived at Atascadero on February 9, 2015. Joan was still euphoric from this most welcome change of circumstance, but her joy would be short lived. The following day, she received an email from the Detctive at the Threat Assessment Group. It appeared that Lester would now undergo a certification review by the residential mental health team at Atascadero. This meant Lester would be re-evaluated and a determination would be made to confirm or reverse the original MDO evaluation recommendations. The Detective further advised that if the finding was confirmed, Lester would have the opportunity to appeal. If he were to win his appeal, he would be afforded an annual MDO review to determine if he is fit for placement back into society. At worst, the certification review could reverse the original MDO evaluation recommendations and he would be released on parole. Unfortunately, the Detective from the Threat Assessment Group advised Joan that the Judges had recently been reversing a number of determinations at appeal.

Joan was gutted and was again left to wait it out. Nearly three months would pass before she finally had an answer: Lester wouldn't be free just yet.

The second round of Lester's MDO evaluations confirmed the recommendations of the first. He would be staying at Atascadero for a little bit longer. At the time of writing this book, Lester has not appealed this finding. Unless he is committed to receive further treatment, he is due for release on February 7, 2019.

It was welcome news, but Joan has learned never to get too excited. She has accepted that her sense of security will always be measured. So she has simply gotten on with living her life. By now, her thirteenth grandchild was born and she was immersing herself in family and new hobbies that she had always wanted to try. This has included her ongoing volunteer work with a national advocacy group for neglected and abused children. She describes this work as her most rewarding yet, as everyday she is inspired by the resolve and courage of the children she meets. For her, it serves as a constant reminder that no matter how difficult life becomes, there is always someone else whose sufferance is worse.

In July 2015, Joan was contacted by Senator Anderson's office and asked to share her story and describe how the Senator had helped her. The invitation was an honor and she eagerly accepted. She met the Senator's aide and a film crew at Senator Anderson's local office in El Cajon and they asked her a series of questions. After the interview the Senator's aide was openly crying. She told Joan that it was cases like hers that made her proud to go to work everyday and made her job feel worthwhile. The aide then presented Joan with a beautifully framed Certificate of Appreciation from the Senator. It read: 'In special recognition of your unyielding dedication to informing the public of the resources available through elected officials and the importance of civic engagement in our community.' Joan was humbled and expressed her deep gratitude to both her and the Senator for their considerable efforts to help her, but felt certain her words could never be enough. She hugged her tightly and they promised to stay in touch.[6]

A few weeks later, Joan organized a lunch with the Senator's aide, Marian and the Detective from the Threat Assessment Group: three amazing women who did so much for her and never received a penny in return. It was Joan's hope not only to thank them, but to also forge a forceful alliance to lobby judicial change in favor of victims like herself.

6   At the time of writing, the video of Joan's interview with Senator Joel Anderson's office has not yet been made publicly available. Please check his website for further details: http://anderson.cssrc.us.

As of now Marian and Joan are working together with Senator Anderson to strengthen sentencing regimes for repeat offenders like Lester. While she hopes Lester will never be released, Joan knows she has precious little time to make some very tough decisions about her future: her work, her family, her life. And so, with a sense of calm that she hasn't known for nearly half of her life, she has started making them, one by one.

She remains busy rebuilding her life and advocating for victims of crime.

JOAN REFLECTS

Despite the pain of this whole ordeal, I have made some wonderful friends.

Howard Bradley, you will always be my knight in shining armor. You believed me when no one else would. Chuck Nachand, you have been my loyal friend and advisor, and gave me hope when I had none. Marian Birge, you are an angel sent from heaven. With nothing to gain, you fought for me over and over until we had an answer. You will forever be my hero. I thank the Threat Assessment Group; you did everything in your power to make sure my family and I would be safe. You are a true beacon of the law enforcement fraternity. Detective Wood, your tenacity and professionalism are appreciated more than you know. To Senator Joel Anderson and your staff, without your help I have no doubt that Lester would be out loose looking for an opportunity to strike again.

Thanks to each of you. I will be forever grateful. I feel privileged to call you my friends.

To Mark, I wonder if you ever regret agreeing to marry into this mess! You have been my rock. Without your love and support, I don't know how I would have made it out the other side.

To my children, you are my greatest achievement. There were so many dark moments in this very long chapter of our lives. At times, you were the only things that kept me hanging on. I am beyond blessed to be your mom.

And last, but certainly not least, thank you to Jackie and Simon for telling my story.

Joan.

Jean Bennett and her girls in their Sunday best.
From left to right: Jayme, Joan, Julia, Jinger, Connie
(Janelle had not yet been born).

Joan and Joe in Mission Bay, San Diego, 1976.

Joan and Jackie, 1978. Several months later the Eigners moved to Via Francis Street.

Joan, Joe and Jackie playing in the front yard of Via Francis Street, 1979. That same year Lester's family moved next door.

Camping in Yosemite, 1988 – the year Lester started stalking Joan. From left to right: Jackie, Joe, Juliann.

The Eigners, 1989. From left to right: Akira, Joe, Joan, Jackie Juliann.

Joan and Sadie at eight weeks old. She was already thirty pounds and would reach a whooping one hundred and twenty pounds full grown. She was Joan's greatest and most loyal protector until her untimely death at just four years old.

Joan and Sadie reuniting after returning from a four-week holiday.

Joe, Jackie and their friends in the Eigners' backyard.
The fence bordering Lester's backyard can be seen on the right.
The 7/11 and taco shop are across the street (7/11 sign visible
behind traffic light).

Joan and Mark, 2011.

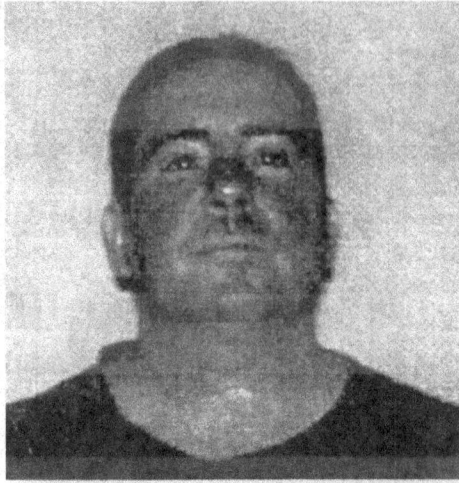

Lester Lyle Worthington depicted in a photo used by the LMSV School District to warn Joan's coworkers.

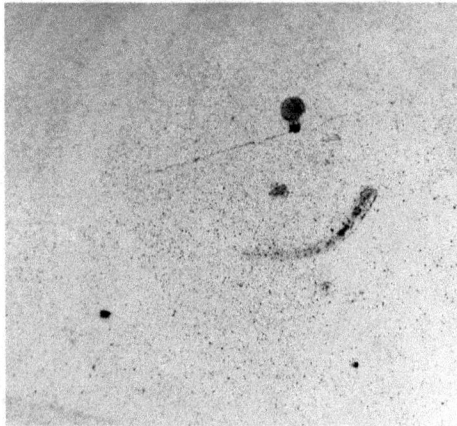

Remnants of the smiley face drawn in green ink on Joan's mailbox in 2009. In 2011, Detective Wood told Joan that the marking was believed to be Lester's 'signature' mark. By then, the drawing had faded significantly, but she was able to take this photo for authorities.

Senate

CERTIFICATE OF RECOGNITION

JOAN WALTERS

IN HONOR OF

OUTSTANDING SERVICE

In special recognition of your unyielding dedication to informing the public of the resources available through elected officials and the importance of civic engagement in our community.

Senator Joel Anderson
July 31, 2015

Certificate of Recognition issued to Joan from Senator Joel Anderson, 2015. Joan remains exceptionally grateful for the Senator's assistance and hopes to continue working with his office to help victims of crime.

(1)

KENNETH E. MARTONE
Clerk of the Superior Court
1994
By: EL CAJON, CA

Court's Ex. A
Case # ELR7698
Rec'd
Dept 7 Clk

Your Honor

Good Morning MAM! I would like To explaine The perdichment 'm IN Now, From my side! The INcidents From lAST year vill Be summarized. Besides The oh going Feude, WHICH JTARTED iN 1987. WHICH WAS AFTer AN AFAir WiTH me AND JOAN. WHICH STARTED, iN 85T286 Words Were excauzed BeTween He HusBenD AND me. Now IN 88, JoAN Filed Burslary CHArges WHicH Were FAlse, AND I WAS ADmonisHed. THe TruTH of THe mATTer s SHe CAlled me over, To sTop The Tension BeTween me AnD THe 'usBenD, AND iN 92 THe SoN Joined iN THe VerBAl JousTs WiTH 'He FATHer. Now! THe FirsT iNciDenT FeB 14 1993 I WAS Almost IN A HeAD on ColisioN. AND INADverTenTly swerveD JusT missing Two peDesTriens By 12 FeeT. WicH TurneD ouT To Be, 'iss JAckie eisner. AFTer THis INciDenT IN WicH I WAsenT ArresTeD THAT NighT. I WAS ASKeD By DeTecTive HounAD — — BruDly To give my siDe. THis TApeD inTerview WAS oN FeB 23 '3. BuT THe resTrAining orDer, Civil suiT, AnD AssAulT CHArge 'As FileD oN FeB 18 1993. I WAS NoT merenDizeD, Nor WAS I TolD F THe CAse PenDing AgAinsT me. IF You lisTen To THe TApe He 'AiD He WAs GunnA Tell Her To File. So AFTer A monTHs Time I Go To CourT, AND subsequenTly ArresTeD, Now JuDge 'iANciAi A CiVAl JuDge gAve me A 250:000 DollAr BAil Becaus of Joan's BoyFrienD, (He explane lATer iN my reporT!) IN WicH He 'AD No righT, I WAS TolD By All 3 of my lAwyers. So We 'o To CourT on THe FirsT INciDenT AND THAT sAme DAy THis 'HArge WAS reDuceD To A misDAmeNer! So THe Very NexT DAy JoAN sAid I TrieD To run Her oFF THe roAD. So 2 DAy's lATer, Her BoyFrienD is ArresTing me AT Work

②

And Again! Her BoyFriend Influenced Judge (Bianclini) To Place Me on Just/y 250,000 Dollar Bail Again. Now! After The 2nd Alleged incident Nothing wasent Filed Again For 1 1/2 monthS (Doctrin of latches) so The Day For court And Still nothing Filed! I Went For A Ducille ride THAT Day. Then Here comes Joan WITH 4 Cameras IN Her Face. Passing me A Total of 5 Times And on Her last Pass She Almost runs me over on pourpous! So I Went Straight Home And Called THe Santee Sherrifs To File A report. I WAs Denied Because She Tried To run me over IN el Cajon And Not Santee. So on My Way out The Dead end Here Comes Her BoyFriend only minuts After My Call To The Santee SherriFs To Tell Her My aligations. The el Cajon Police Did Take My report And Theors An Actual Case # number AgAinsT JoAn For Assault With A Deadly Weapon. And Through Brodlys checking my report out IM Given THe Charge of Stalking! (And yes) iTs Filed 2 Days After my Assault CHarge. Now! THe Time comes To Go To court For my Second Assault CHarge on JoAn And JoAn (States under oath) THaT She DiDnT Believe I Was Breaking restraining orders. But! She Felt I Was on My Way To Her Work!!!, These Are Her very Words, AT evidencery Hearing. And Becaus I lost My JoB And couldnT Pay THe lawyer 5,000 more He HaD HimselF Dissmissed From The case Which Was unJustly GrAnTeD By Judge Hudsnour so Now I GeT A Public PreTender To DeFend Me I Sell my Truck For THe 50,000 Bail. So Now I'm looking For work. But! THis Time Im Keeping A log of Times + Places of my Whereabouts. THen Here is JoAns BoyFriend By

③

My SCHOOL To see WHAT IM Driving! I Have Witnesses
To THIS, And THe Very NexT DAY, JOAN STATes IM Across
Her Bus yard. THen CHanges Her STATment! THAT I Passed
Her Going THe opposite Direction, No uHere Near Her
Work or my Home so I Have To Go To CourT THe NexT
DAY wich I Did And Have always Done my BAil is
increases To 100.000. so THe Judge Binds me over
And Here ive Been IN Jail since my BroTHer Come up
with 12.500 $ For A Good lawyer. Because THe PuBlic DeFF-
ender DiDnT Bring in my witnesses AT THe Hotel. VeriFying
my STAy THere At THe very Time Joan says I'm going THe
opposite Direction. THese Are Hotel emphyees wich were
crucial To my whereAbouts AT THAT CerTin Time. so AFTer
Being in JAil my 3rd lawyer was allowed To replace THe
PuBlic PreTender. Now! THe Trial ronald stout DiD
real good And Hung THe Jury. BuT! THe D'A wHo Hase
Token THis Case Personally! Asked me To still Be Bound
over wHich Brings us To You! Now You allow Hearsay
evidence wich would PAinT me To Be oF BAd CHaricter.
Plus Brodly Heartising me on THe INSiDe, And AFTer Being
Broken AFTer confinmenT, I suprised my lawyer
THAT morning And Pleaded GuilTy. BuT I was IN
THe BelieFe THAT I was Pleading, To AssaulT NoT
STAlking! THis is THe GoD's TruTH Your Honor. so AFTer
THAT morning, I Told my lawyer some lawyer-ClienT
confidensibleTies you Know BeTween me And Him.
I would Have Never Pleaded To STAlking. Becous my Civil
lawyers Advises me THAT would HurT my CounTer
Civil suiT AgAinst JoAn, For my DAmeges! THe NexT

(4)

DAY I Found out my mistake And Told my lawyer
I wished To CHange my Plea, So When we see you
AGAin IN Court my lawyer Tells me IN THe Back
room THAT THere is A conflict of interest And He
Will Be Asking you To Be Dismissed From THe case
Well I Didn't Want A Public Deffender so I Back
off. He said it in my Best interest To Keep THe Deal
And you'll Give me Time served of 6 months 20 Days
THen on THe Day of sentincing He THen Tells me
THAT THe Deal is reneged. So I Would Also
like To renege THe Deal! With A reversal of
my Plea. Back To innocent! And let THe People
of THis Great Judicial system Decide my
innocence. By A Jury Trial In wich I Believe
is my right without undo Pressure By my lawyer
And I Would Also Beg THe Court not To Dismisse
mr Stout. As my lawyer. or! A 4TH lawyer
of my CHoosing At THe County's expense! Just like
Stout's County Payment For His services His
Motion Before THe second Trial was I shouldn't
Have To Pay His services Twice. or A lawyer
of His calliber At my CHoosing. So I Wish To
Pleade innocent And Beg not To let Stout out
THank you your Honor For your Time And
consideration on THis matter
                    Sincerly
            Lester Worthington

Also your Honore!

About Detective Bradly, He Hase Been Way To Byass To Performe His Duty Without Prejudece! The Things He's Done on This Case ① The Interview Already Fibling Then Telling me He's Guna Have Joan File. ② He's Been To Her House About 60 To 65 Times. ③ She's Been To His House on several occasions. ④ He's Checked on Wants And Warents on my entire Family, subsuquently Arresting my Brother Chris For An old Charge In wich CDF Would Not except His Booking ⑤ He's Brought Christmas presents To The eighers And Children To play with Theres. ⑥ He's Been at All Hearngs I mean All And even Testifies For Her Behalf. ⑦ The mans A Thief I Have proof By my privet investigator That He's stolden From The County. ⑧ He's Been To Byass one of my civil counts of (Doctrin of unclean Hands) ⑨ He Testified under oath That He hosent met John Before Feb 14 93 But! my privet Investigator Found out They Have Been Going To The same Church For 4 years Now?. All These reasons is Why The D.A Hosent used Him Hos A witness But Hes on The witness list For The People. All These reasons To me your Honor Seem past The scope of Being impersnal And clearly Show Him To Be Byass For Joan?!. Thank you Again your Honor! ☺

PART THREE: STALKING RESOURCES

One of the reasons we wrote this book is to help the public, police, lawyers, and the Judiciary to have a better understanding of stalking, the impact on victims, and how victims can be better protected and assisted. Accordingly, we have included the following chapters to assist in this regard and to serve in educating and informing the reader. Details of sources used and referred to can be found at pages 175–178.

What is stalking?

Stalking is more than just unwanted attention or unrequited feelings. It is invasive, constant, unrelenting and crippling. Stalking isn't just about celebrities and it doesn't discriminate. It is a crime that doesn't consider age, occupation, social status, wealth, ethnicity or sexual orientation. It is about everyday people and the offenders who want to hurt them.

Stalking episodes can last for days, weeks, months or even years. The average stalking experience lasts around two years, and can involve a range of illegal or unwanted acts including harassing phone calls, surveillance, sending letters or gifts, vandalism, theft, assault, rape, and in the most extreme cases, murder. In fact, about one in three stalkers will become violent toward their victim at some stage. In an attempt to cause maximum harm to a victim, stalkers may also target family members, friends, co-workers, or even a victim's pet. If a stalker is unable to harass a victim—for example, because a court order is in effect—they may ask or employ someone else to do it on their behalf.

Stalking is more common than most people know. Attempts to understand the true extent of stalking have been made through studies conducted in a number of countries, including Australia, Canada, New Zealand, the United Kingdom, and the US. In short, about one in five people will be stalked in their lifetime. Other common characteristics of stalking include:

- most offenders are male and are known to their victim in some capacity
- individuals who are divorced or separated are at a higher risk of stalking
- there is a strong link between stalking and domestic violence
- nearly half of victims fear for their future
- restraining orders are often violated or ineffective at stopping stalking, and
- many victims never report their abuse to police, and for those who do, few cases result in criminal prosecution.

Stalkers offend for a range of reasons. For some, it is a way to exert power over their victim, or punish them for leaving the relationship or rejecting them. For others, it fulfills a desire for intimacy or lust. Some offenders simply want to control the victim's life. Since the criminalization of stalking, there has been a sharp rise in interest in the subject of stalkers, and researchers and professionals from various disciplines have sought to understand the motivations of stalkers. Unfortunately, the only definitive thing that all of this research has uncovered is that stalkers come from all walks of life and intelligence levels. Possibly the most widely recognized tool to classify stalker motivation and risk is known as the Stalking Risk Profile. The Stalking Risk Profile is discussed in more depth in the chapter titled *Why Stalkers Stalk*.

With the uptake of technology and access to the internet, the use of technologies and social media by stalkers—or 'cyber stalking'—is increasing. Current figures suggest about one in four stalking victims experience some form of cyber stalking or abuse, but this is likely to rise significantly. For stalkers, the internet is a tool to get information, enact their fantasies, spread malicious lies, make threats, or even identify and interact with new victims. It can intensify in chat rooms where stalkers systematically flood the victim's inbox with obscene, hateful, or threatening messages and images. A cyber stalker may further assume the identity of his or her victim and post salacious, demeaning and offensive information in the cyber community. Cyber stalkers may use information acquired online to further intimidate, harass, and threaten their victim via courier mail, phone calls, and physically appearing at a residence or work place.

WHAT IS THE IMPACT OF STALKING ON VICTIMS?

Stalking victims have been a rich source of information for researchers and there is a growing body of work that is contributing to the understanding of the experience of protracted harassment and stalking. The effects of stalking victimization are becoming better understood through self-reporting surveys and smaller studies of specific victim groups. Apart from the frequent legal prerequisite of fear, and the possibility of injury due to assault, research has shown that victims suffer a wide range of psychological, physical, occupational, social and general lifestyle effects as a consequence of being stalked. As with so many aspects of stalking, the experience and impact can vary greatly between victims. Behaviors that are considered annoying to one victim can have a shattering effect on another.

Stalking can change a person, and quite often it does. Only those who have experienced it can truly understand. It can ruin relationships, friendships and impact the lives of those close to a victim. It can result in serious economic and social difficulties for victims; and in many cases, victims are forced to quit their job or place of education, move house (either temporarily or permanently), move to another country, change their appearance or name, and take significant security precautions whenever leaving home. In many cases, victims become socially withdrawn and avoid social contact altogether. In one study, stalking victims reported taking the following evasive actions in response to their victimization:

- eighty one per cent changed their telephone number
- sixty five per cent took additional security measures
- sixty three per cent avoided social outings
- forty four per cent relocated
- forty per cent went 'underground'
- thirty nine per cent quit their job or worked less
- twenty one per cent changed jobs.

Astonishingly, nineteen per cent of victims either assaulted their stalker (many in self-defense) or had someone else assault their stalker for them.

The impacts of stalking can be varied and extreme. They can vary according to a victim's characteristics, past experience, current circumstances, and what they know or don't know about the stalker. How others respond to the victim's situation, including how the stalking is managed by authorities, can influence the overall effect that the stalking episode has on the victim. Although female victims usually report greater levels of fear, studies have found that males subjected to stalking experience similar symptoms to those reported by their female counterparts.

Victims of stalking are two to three times more likely to suffer from psychological distress. This includes victims experiencing a greater degree of distrust, suspicion, caution, fear, nervousness, anger, paranoia, depression and introversion. These behaviors and feelings are seen in various common symptoms of stress, such as chronic sleep and appetite disturbance, excessive tiredness, weakness, tension, headaches, and persistent nausea. Sadly, many stalking victims will experience drastic changes to their personality, and some will consider or attempt suicide. In fact, thirty-seven per cent of stalking victims fulfill the criteria for Post-Traumatic Stress Disorder. This is the same condition that is experienced by members of the military or first responders who see the worst in humanity during war or emergencies.

Although not exhaustive, the following are some of the more common effects that victims of stalking experience:

Effects on mental health

- Denial, confusion, self-doubt, questioning if what is happening is unreasonable, wondering if they are overreacting.
- Frustration.
- Guilt, embarrassment, self-blame.
- Apprehension, fear, terror of being alone or that they, others or pets will be harmed.
- Feeling isolated and helpless to stop the harassment.
- Depression (all symptoms related to depression).
- Anxiety, panic attacks, agoraphobia (frightened to leave the house, never feeling safe).
- Difficulty concentrating, attending and remembering things.
- Inability to sleep—nightmares, ruminating.
- Irritability, anger, homicidal thoughts.
- Emotional numbing.
- Symptoms of Post-Traumatic Stress Disorder e.g. hyper-vigilance (always on the lookout), flashbacks of frightening incidents, easily startled.
- Insecurity and inability to trust others, problems with intimacy.
- Personality changes due to becoming more suspicious, introverted or aggressive.
- Self-medication alcohol/ drugs or using prescribed medications.
- Suicidal thoughts and/or suicide attempts.

Effects on physical health

- Fatigue from difficulty sleeping, being constantly on guard, symptoms of depression.
- Effects of chronic stress including headaches, hypertension.
- Gastrointestinal problems.
- Fluctuations in weight due to not eating or comfort eating.
- Development or exacerbation of pre-existing conditions e.g. asthma, gastric ulcers and psoriasis.
- Dizziness.
- Shortness of breath.
- Impact on health of increased use of alcohol, cigarettes or drugs.
- Sexual dysfunction.
- Physical injury due to not concentrating or being under the influence of substances.
- Heart palpitations and sweating.

Effects on work and school

- Deteriorating school/work performance.
- Increased sick leave.
- Leaving job or being sacked.
- Changing career.
- Dropping out of school—poorer education and career opportunities.

Effects on social life

- Insecurity and inability to trust others impacting on current and future relationships and friendships.
- Problems with physical and emotional intimacy.
- Avoidance of usual activities e.g., going to the gym, going out.
- Isolation through trying to protect others, feeling misunderstood or psychological symptoms.

- Others withdrawing from the victim because they don't believe the victim, they are unable to cope with the victim's mental state or as a direct consequence of third-party victimization.
- Victim moving to a new area, changing their phone number, name or even their appearance.

Effects on finances

- Loss of wages due to sick leave, leaving job or changing career.
- Costs incurred through legal fees.
- Expense of increasing home and personal security.
- Cost involved in repairing property damage.
- Seeking psychological counseling and medical treatment.
- Cost involved in breaking leases on rented properties.
- Expense of relocation.

Victims of stalking do not always report their abuse. For those that don't, they are usually too afraid to upset their stalker—fearing reporting to authorities will only serve to heighten the harassment; or worse, fearing the police will not believe or help them. Most stalking victims believe that the justice or mental health systems fail them. For victims, this can include displays of disbelief or powerlessness by the police, insufficient evidence to pursue the offender or for a successful prosecution, unresponsiveness or incompetence of mental health professionals, and a failure to stop the stalker through traditional means such as restraining orders, police warnings, arrests, convictions, or even imprisonment. In fact, many victims are forced to take action themselves, but unfortunately, evasive action very rarely stops the stalker. This is why so many victims experience a strong sense of helplessness and feel like nothing works.

THE HISTORY OF STALKING

Stalking is not a new phenomenon. In fact, stalking-like behaviors have existed in society for a long time. Some researchers even suggest that they are commonly glorified through romantic notions of passionate love pursuits in popular film and media. So when legislators began to put a criminal label on this type of conduct, it was exceptionally controversial. They would face great difficulty in framing legal sanctions because when viewed in isolation, a lot of stalking behavior is ostensibly routine and harmless, like sending gifts or walking on the same street as the victim.

Until stalking became a crime, obsessive behavior was considered to be a mental health issue and not within the domain of law enforcement. Effective legal action or intervention almost always required the victim to be physically harmed, or at the very least have their property damaged. Not only was this completely inadequate, but it also did not consider the emotional and mental harm caused by the persistent fear and apprehension of being stalked.

ORIGINS OF STALKING IN THE LAW

In the legal context, some of the earliest documented cases show that English courts addressed stalking-like behavior as early as the eighteenth century. For example, in 1704, a man named Dr. Lane persistently pursued a young woman named Miss Dennis. He would repeatedly follow and harass her and even attempted to enter her bedroom one evening. On one occasion, he followed her while she traveled to London with her mother. Once there, he rented an adjacent room at an inn where the women were staying and assaulted a man who was accompanying them. He would later assault Miss Dennis's Barrister, severely beating him with a cane. This act would finally see him detained by police and tried before the courts. The Judge ordered Dr. Lane to provide four hundred pounds as security to ensure he would 'keep the peace' for one year.

In another detailed English case from 1840, a Barrister named Richard Dunn pursued his victim, Angela Coutts, for nearly a year. He had never met Miss Coutts, but he developed a strong fixation with her nonetheless. Initially, he would send her two letters to express his desires, but Miss Coutts threw them away and did not reply. Undeterred, he followed her to a hotel where she was staying, snuck into her room and left his business card inside. She then moved to another hotel.

Spurred on by the rejection, Mr. Dunn bombarded her with letters and frequently approached her in public. She subsequently began using a male servant to provide protection from Mr. Dunn. Then one of his letters would finally scare her into seeking assistance from the courts. Mr. Dunn was later apprehended and ordered to produce two separate payments of five hundred pounds as security to keep the peace. Unable to provide these sureties, he was placed into custody at York Castle until his court matter was heard. But because Miss Coutts left the jurisdiction, he was soon released.

As soon as he was free, Mr. Dunn continued his pursuit. He followed Miss Coutts, sent her letters and packages, kept her under surveillance and would accost her on the street, at church and on vacation. She again feared for her safety and applied for a warrant to apprehend him. The warrant was granted and he was again placed into custody because he could not provide sureties of peace. For reasons unknown, he was soon released and he immediately began harassing Miss Coutts again. He sent her a letter asking to meet, stating: 'If you refuse this request, you will, when it is too late, repent a course, the consequences of which will sooner or later fall on yourself and your family.'

She again sought recourse from the courts, but they determined that her application was insufficient and the charges against Mr. Dunn were dismissed. In making their finding, the Judges at least possessed the insight to recognize and reproach the inherent inadequacies in the law to address stalking-like behaviors and their impact on victims.

Stalking was not recognized as a crime for another one hundred and fifty years. It took the progressive state of California to pave the way. In 1990, California passed the first anti-stalking legislation in the world. However, as so often is the case a local tragedy would provide the catalyst for lawmakers to act. While many ordinary women were being harmed and killed by their stalkers, it was the high profile cases of two popular celebrities, Theresa Saldana and Rebecca Schaeffer, that ultimately forced legislators into action.

CELEBRITY STALKING CASES

In 1982, Theresa survived a vicious murder attempt by her stalker Arthur Richard Jackson. Jackson, a drifter from Scotland, developed his obsession with the actress after seeing her in the 1980 films Defiance and Raging Bull. His attack was calculating and premeditated. In 1982, he entered the US illegally and hired a private investigator to find Theresa. He quickly obtained her mother's unlisted phone number and, posing as the assistant to the world-renowned filmmaker, Martin Scorsese, contacted Theresa's mother to obtain Theresa's address.

Jackson approached Theresa outside her West Hollywood residence and stabbed her ten times with a fourteen centimeter hunting knife and nearly killed her. The stabbing frenzy was so fierce that it bent the blade of the knife. The attack was only stopped when a deliveryman heard Theresa's cries and courageously intervened and subdued Jackson.

Theresa needed surgery on her heart and lungs as well as twenty-six pints of blood, but she would live. Jackson was convicted for the attack and served fourteen years in prison. Upon his release, he was extradited to the United Kingdom for robbery and murder and he would die in prison in 2004. Interestingly, a look into his past reveals that he also made threats to former US President John F. Kennedy and was subsequently arrested and deported to Scotland in 1961.

Jackson's method of finding Theresa Saldana would later inspire the stalker Robert John Bardo to hire a private investigator to contact Rebecca Schaeffer, a young actress whom he subsequently murdered in 1989.

Rebecca Schaffer was the talented and beautiful young star of the television series *My Sister Sam*. Bardo had become obsessed with Rebecca after the previous target of his obsession, child peace activist Samantha Smith, died in a plane crash four years earlier. In 1987, he travelled to Los Angeles hoping to meet Rebecca, but he was turned away by security guards working at the Warner Bros studios where she was filming. A month later, he tried again. This time he was armed with a knife, but the guards managed to keep him away from the actress. He then returned to his native town of Tucson, Arizona (about seven hours drive from Los Angeles) and focused his affections on pop singers Debbie Gibson and Tiffany (Tiffany Renee Darwish), both of whom were wildly popular at the time.

By 1989, Mr. Bardo's obsession with Rebecca was reignited, and he travelled to Los Angeles for a third time. Before he left, he hired a private detective to locate her address. When he arrived in her neighborhood, he roamed the streets and tried to confirm her address with a neighbor. When he was confident he had the right apartment, he finally knocked on her door. Rebecca answered and they had a short conversation. He showed her a letter that she had previously autographed for him. Spooked, she asked him not to return and shut the door.

He returned an hour later and again knocked on her apartment door. This time she answered with what Mr. Bardo later described as 'a cold look on her face'. He removed his gun from a brown paper bag and shot her in the chest. Rebecca managed to scream before collapsing in her doorway and Mr. Bardo fled. A neighbor rang the paramedics and Rebecca was taken to a hospital, but she died thirty minutes later. She was only twenty-one years old.

The next day, Mr. Bardo was seen running through traffic on a busy highway in his hometown of Tucson. The police were called and he was arrested on the spot. He later confessed to the murder.

NON-CELEBRITY STALKING MURDERS

While Rebecca's death ignited widespread public intrigue and outrage over the gaps in existing laws to deal with stalking, four other Orange County women would also be slain by their stalker within seven months of her death. These women were all murdered by former boyfriends or husbands, and three of the victims had a restraining order against their killer when they died. These women were not celebrities like Theresa or Rebecca and perhaps their deaths alone would not have gathered the volume of support required to change or enact laws. Yet their deaths were mourned as much as any and the impact of their loss was felt just the same.

The first of these victims was nineteen year old Tammy Marie Davis. She was shot to death by Brian Keith Framstead, her ex-boyfriend and the father of their twenty-one month old daughter. Only weeks before she died, Tammy Marie begged the police to help her, asking 'What does he have to do, shoot me?' Family members and friends all stated that the couple had a tumultuous relationship involving previous episodes of violence. She had even obtained a restraining order against Mr. Framstead in the months before her attack. In fact, he was due to serve a six month term in jail for breaching that order only days after he killed her.

On the night of her murder, Tammy Marie cowered in the doorway of a darkened home and screamed for help as Mr. Framstead pursued her. As she banged on the door of a stranger's home, he pulled his shotgun's trigger at pointblank range and killed her. He fled the scene, but was eventually identified and pursued by police. About nineteen hours after he killed Tammy Marie, he set himself on fire while being chased by California Highway Patrol officers.

The second victim was Narges 'Manijeh' Bolouri. She was a thirty-four year old Iranian-born nurse. She was stalked by her ex-boyfriend, Hossein Ghaffari, for ten years before he burned her to death. His obsession even spanned continents as he followed Manijeh from Austria to America to continue his pursuit. While her relatives never met Mr. Ghaffari, they knew that he had been harassing her for eighteen months before he finally killed her. He repeatedly told her that he would kill her if she married someone else. When Mr. Ghaffari learned of Manijeh's plans to marry a doctor from San Diego, he drove to her home, parked his car and waited for her.

At nine o'clock in the morning, she climbed into her car and shut the door. She was on her way to work. Seconds later, Mr. Ghaffari gunned his engine and rammed her car with his own. Before she could move, he covered her car in petrol and set it alight. Within minutes, Manijeh was dead from smoke inhalation and had suffered fourth degree burns to over ninety per cent of her body. No one even heard her scream.

Immediately afterward, Mr. Ghaffari ran to the front door of Manijeh's home, leaving a trail of blood on the sidewalk and a bloody handprint on the front gate. Relatives told police that he was pounding on the door and shouting, 'I have killed your daughter!'

Days later, twenty six year old former Swiss Olympic skier, Patricia Kastle, was shot in the head by her former husband, just five weeks after she divorced him. Only one week before she died, she told a friend that she was planning to move from Orange County to get away from her ex-husband. Sadly, she delayed her move because she feared his reaction. Friends of the couple described her ex-husband as neurotic and insecure, and said he repeatedly accused Patricia of cheating on him. He often called the shop that Patricia owned and threatened the lives of the women who worked there, and he told a neighbor of his plans to kill both Patricia and himself.

Overcome by his grief and anger after Patricia left him, he tracked her down one day and started shooting. She fled through the grounds of a mobile home park screaming for someone to save her and eventually a male resident let her into his trailer. Moments later, Patricia's ex-husband then burst into the trailer, shoved the other man to the ground and threatened to kill him. During the altercation, Patricia escaped through the back door, but her ex-husband quickly caught up with her and shoved her to the ground. He fired several bullets into her head.

Two weeks later, Brenda Lee Albright-Thurman became the fourth victim. She was gunned down by her ex-boyfriend, Rodney Terry Cornegay, after he hired a private investigator to find her. Before her death, she frequently complained that Mr. Cornegay was breaking into her apartment and vandalizing her car. She had even obtained a restraining order against him, but he repeatedly breached it.

On the morning that she died, Mr. Cornegay smashed a window and entered her apartment. She managed to run outside but he chased after her and began firing shots. As he was shooting, police arrived at the scene, but Brenda had already sustained fatal injuries and she died three hours later. When Mr. Cornegay saw police, he turned the gun on himself and committed suicide.

POLITICIANS FINALLY TAKE ACTION

By now, newspapers were awash with articles detailing the powerlessness of law enforcement to combat stalking crimes that were taking the lives of innocent victims. In response, Municipal

Court Judge John Watson began drafting the world's first anti-stalking legislation. When he was finished, Judge Watson presented the statute to California State Senator Edward Royce and in September 1990, the state legislature enacted California Penal Code Section 646.9 'Stalking'.

The offence of stalking was defined as:

> any person who willfully, maliciously, and repeatedly follows or harasses another person and who makes a credible threat with the intent to place that person in reasonable fear of death or great bodily harm.

'Harass' was defined as:

> a knowing and willful course of conduct directed at a specific person which seriously alarms, annoys or harasses the person, and which serves no legitimate purpose. The course of conduct must be such as would cause a reasonable person to suffer substantial emotional distress to the person. Course of conduct means a pattern of conduct composed of a series of acts over a period of time, however short, evidencing a continuity of purpose.

Within three years of the passage of legislation in California, all fifty states and the District of Columbia had introduced anti-stalking laws or amended their criminal codes to address stalking-like behavior. This relatively rapid succession was due in no small part to the testimony of witnesses at state legislature hearings that were held around the country. Hundreds of victims came forward to share their story and describe what it was like to 'live in the vise of a stalker's obsession.'

These hearings provided a compelling insight for the judiciary into how stalkers destroyed lives and how authorities were often powerless to act until things turned violent. One witness testified:

> the police were not insensitive, but they were stymied. The man violated almost every area of my life, but he had broken no law. The police worked with me to prevent an assault but, in the final analysis said there was nothing they could do till

an assault occurred.

Another witness described how her daughter had been harassed and terrorized for eight years by a male with a mental illness. She detailed how this ordeal had changed their lives:

> There is no way to describe to you the fear that our family has had of this individual, no way to describe what it is like to live a life constantly being on guard. Kimberley, her dad, and I all suffer from stress-related symptoms ... Despite the threats ..., despite his repeated violations of restraining orders, despite the professional assessment of him as dangerous, both the district attorney and our attorney have said that nothing can be done until Doe does something. What is the something that they must wait for him to do—kidnap Kimberley, rape Kimberley, or kill her? Would you be willing to sit back and wait for that to happen to your son or daughter?'

In 1993, Kathleen Krueger, the wife of US Senator Bob Krueger used her own experiences as a stalking victim to campaign for federal anti-stalking laws. Subsequently, the US Congress legislated to prohibit interstate stalking and malicious communication when it passed the *Communications Decency Act 1995* and the *Interstate Stalking Punishment and Prevention Act 1996*.

On May 24, 1991, Mark David Bleakley would become the first person to be arrested for stalking in California after his ex-girlfriend complained to the police of his continued harassment. She alleged that he made repeated threats to hurt her, continually rang her home, poured acid on her car, slashed her car tires and stole her dog. When police took Mr. Bleakley into custody, they also located a .357 magnum revolver in his apartment. He would later be convicted of stalking and sentenced to one year in prison and six months in a rehabilitation facility.

While the introduction of anti-stalking legislation was warmly welcomed by victims and their advocates, debate would continue among the legal fraternity as to whether the laws provided sufficient clarity and regard for constitutional rights. So in 1993, the US Congress commissioned the National Institute of Justice to develop a model stalking code to help support and guide the states in drafting and enforcing their respective statutes. In doing this, the National Institute of Justice pulled together criminal justice practitioners, victim advocates and legislators across the country, but their efforts were largely unsuccessful.

While the model code did provide some much needed assistance to state legislators, few stalking cases would be investigated or prosecuted in the early years after the statutes were passed. Police blamed a lack of reporting by stalking victims and difficulties in collecting solid evidence needed to charge a suspect. Prosecutors also found it hard to secure convictions because Judges and juries often knew very little about the crime of stalking.

Despite the passage of time and a significantly greater awareness of the crime of stalking, responding to and preventing this offence remains a challenge. One of the continued difficulties is in ensuring frontline responders like police patrol officers and crisis workers are adequately trained in stalking laws and victimization. Another major challenge is the hesitation of some prosecutors to pursue stalking cases. Some may feel that they don't have enough evidence to secure a win at trial and they may not want to risk losing.

Yet, the offence of stalking has stood the test of time. Stalking is now criminalized in a number of countries, including Australia, Canada, the United Kingdom (including England, Wales and Scotland), France, Italy, Japan, Germany, Netherlands, and most recently India, who changed their penal code in 2013 to include stalking offences. While anti-stalking laws are not a cure, they attempt to tilt the balance away from the stalker and towards those who need protection the most: the victims and their families.

WHY STALKERS STALK

Offenders are 'tortured' by the all-consuming thoughts of their victim.
They do not do anything without thinking of their victim: when
they brush their teeth, they think of their victim; when they eat their
breakfast, they think of their victim. The thoughts of their victims are
as torturous for them as their behavior is for their victim.

Dr. Michelle Ward, Criminal Psychologist

Since the criminalization of stalking in 1990, there has been a sharp rise in interest in the subject of stalkers. Individuals from various disciplines such as psychiatry, psychology, criminology, sociology, public policy, legal professions and police have aimed to better understand the legal and behavioral implications of this crime. This has included research into identifying victims and offenders, offender threat assessments, and risk management.

Many key questions remain unanswered, including what motivates stalkers and how can you predict if they will become violent? While the research may lend little comfort to victims of stalking, it is promising to see the growing body of research and literature into this crime, and its ability to better inform those charged with preventing, investigating and managing it.

In attempting to answer perhaps the most compelling question of all—why do stalkers stalk?—the research is extensive and varied. Researchers suggest there are anywhere between two and seven types of stalkers and have developed different models to explain the various motives for stalking. No one model or 'typology' has been universally accepted by all professionals. Most of the typologies introduced to date make distinctions based on characteristics of the stalker or their victim, while others have focused on the relationship between stalkers and victim.

With offender typologies, issues such as offender mental state are categorized to explain their stalking behavior. For example, they would be labeled as psychopathic or psychotic personality stalkers. With victim typologies, categories are distinguished by victim type or the feeling a stalker has for his victim. This may include things like 'celebrity', 'lust', 'hit' (the stalker has been hired to murder the victim and stalks them to learn their routines), 'love-scorned', 'political', and 'domestic' (the victim is a former partner).

Because so little is known regarding Lester's past, including his mental state (the court appointed psychologist reports were withheld from the authors), Joan has attempted to understand her victimization through popular stalker/victim relationship typologies. As the name implies, these typologies are based on the type of relationship between the stalker and their victim.

The first known study that attempted to classify stalker/victim relationships was likely conducted in 1993. Since this time, there have been plenty more. One thing they all share is a classification system that is inclusive of at least two main categories: stalkers and victims that have been in a prior relationship and those that have not. Resoundingly, victims are more likely to know their stalker and most (approximately fifty-seven per cent) have been in a previous intimate relationship with them. Strangers comprise anywhere between sixteen and twenty-one per cent of cases.

The Stalking Risk Profile is perhaps one of the most complex but widely acknowledged tools around. It was developed to assist mental health professionals and police with understanding and managing stalking behavior. This typology considers things like the context in which the stalking arose, the stalker's initial motivation for contacting the victim, the nature of any prior relationship between the victim and stalker, and the role of mental illness in motivating the stalking behavior. They have classed stalkers into five categories: the Rejected Stalker; the Resentful Stalker; the Intimacy Seeker; the Incompetent Suitor; and the Predatory Stalker

When considering Joan's case, it is difficult to place her example into a specific typology. She and Lester were not quite acquaintances, but Lester was not completely unknown to Joan either. Lester's claim that he had a relationship with Joan provides a far more common explanation for his stalking behavior. Joan often mocks this irony, admitting that she would at least be able to understand Lester's motivation if they had been lovers.

For Joan, the only insight into Lester's psyche would come from an unlikely source. It wasn't long after the 1994 trial verdict that someone who was intimately involved in the case rang her and described some of the alarming findings outlined in Lester's confidential court-ordered psychiatric assessment. Joan knew she wasn't allowed to know the contents of the report, but she listened to the caller describe, among other things, Lester's intense fixation with her and his general hatred of women. She knew the caller was breaching protocol by sharing this information, for which she was grateful, but it still did little to help her understand why Lester had chosen her, or to quell her fears that he may one day hurt her or her kids.

Stalking and violence

Assessing the level of threat posed by a stalker and successfully managing this risk is exceptionally difficult. Human beings are terribly unpredictable and even the best laid plans have little defense to spontaneity and unexplained aggression. Researchers and stalking experts have gone to great lengths to attempt to understand what makes a stalker lethal, and what early warning signs can lead to detection and prevention of violence. Unfortunately, stalking is often an invisible crime until violence results. On average, the duration between stalking and the first episode of violence is five years. Ironically, this is exactly the amount of time between the onset of Lester's harassment and his attempt to run Jackie and Melanie over with his vehicle.

The importance of early identification and response to stalkers cannot be understated. While homicide is believed to occur in only two per cent of stalking cases, a US study found that stalking preceded seventy six per cent of intimate partner murders. Stalkers are addicted to their stalking behavior. They get a 'high' with every reaction they earn from the victim, and soon they can become dependent on the rush. So the stalker goes back for more and more as their need increases. For some, the rush will diminish, and they will need to escalate their actions. Stalkers can be persistent, driven and resourceful. For those stalkers who truly want to hurt their victim, they will readily create or find opportunities to access them. Whether or not the stalker is prepared to go to jail as a result of their actions will more likely influence how overt any physical violence will be.

When Lester first realized that he could scare Joan, it almost certainly empowered and validated him in a way that he had never felt. He would quickly grow addicted to this feeling, and become obsessed with his need to scare and dominate her. And when it wasn't enough to just scare her, he would target the entire family. Lester had become consumed by his 'game', and when he was in full intensity, he had no care or respect for restraining orders or police. Ultimately, Joan will have to look over her shoulder as long as Lester is alive.

Predicting violence in stalkers will likely remain a difficult task. This is because there are so many variables that influence whether a particular individual will become violent or not. This includes social, biological and psychological factors, as well as conscious and unconscious motivations. Plenty of research has attempted to identify the primary variables for proclivity to violence, and to date, the following three are commonly cited as significant and strong predictors: having previous criminal history (particularly interpersonal violence); having a substance or drug dependence; and prior sexual intimacy with the victim.

One of the strongest triggers for violence is actual or perceived rejection of the stalker by the victim. Lester quite openly discussed his feelings of Joan's rejection, both during his testimony in 1994 and in subsequent letters to the court. For stalkers, rejection creates a strong sense of abandonment, deeply wounds self-esteem, and creates overwhelming feelings of shame and humiliation. In response to this acute sense of vulnerability, the stalker becomes engulfed in anger and rage, which often ignites a physical retaliation. The stalker then achieves a sense of power over their victim, and their self-esteem is temporarily restored. Other triggers for violence include an imminent threat felt by the stalker, or intervention by a third party on behalf of the victim.

Mental disorders and stalking

Research is far from definitive when it comes to measuring the number of stalkers who have a mental illness. A review of the research can be confusing and frustrating for readers. It would seem that, depending on what you read, anywhere between fifty and ninety per cent of stalkers suffer some mental disorder. The most common are personality disorders, schizophrenia and other psychotic disorders, depression, and substance use disorders. Of these, personality disorders are most frequently noted—

with clinical studies showing up to fifty per cent of stalkers having been diagnosed with one. Paranoid, dependent, narcissistic and antisocial personality disorders appear to predominate. For most stalkers where a mental disorder is present, the disorder usually contributes to the onset of the stalking behavior. In a significant minority of cases, the stalking behavior occurs as a direct result of psychotic symptoms. Research into the prevalence of various personality disorders in stalkers is ongoing, with two large projects currently underway in Melbourne and New York.

ASSISTING VICTIMS[7]

The victims of stalking need our help, understanding and most importantly our protection. As we have seen from Joan's experience, stalking can have a devastating and shattering impact on one's life and those of their loved ones. All of us have a responsibility to do all that we can to ensure that no other stalking victim goes through what Joan went through. For being stalked can happen to anyone of us. No one is immune to being the subject of a stalker's obsession.

This is not something that we say lightly: Stalking is a daily reality for many thousands of women and a smaller but equally victimized number of men. To be stalked is to be a victim of a crime that transgresses 'all important boundaries that protect individuals from incursions by those that they perceive as threatening.' What we have tried to do in this chapter is offer practical suggestions for victims and make recommendations for

---

7   The information provided in this chapter is general in nature and should
     not be considered as legal advice or applicable to your jurisdiction. This
     is because each jurisdiction may be subject to different laws and law
     enforcement procedures. Most importantly, you should always ensure that
     your safety is paramount. Always seek advice and assistance from your
     local police or prosecution agency.

changes to the law and police and corrections procedure.

While we do not take credit for the suggestions we have outlined in this chapter, we believe that they are fundamental to helping redress the balance in favor of victims of stalking. For far too long, victims have been marginalized by the criminal justice system; regarded as an inconvenience; overlooked in favor of the offender; and, worst of all, made to feel like they are the ones on trial. This must change. No longer must victims be 'broken in so many pieces' by their experience with the criminal justice system.

For those victims (and their family, friends and colleagues) who are confused and bewildered by what is happening to them, we offer the following suggestions that we believe will assist in regaining a sense of empowerment and control over one's life. We also make recommendations for reform to the criminal justice system so that the victims of stalking are placed at the forefront and their welfare and protection are the focus of the police and the judiciary. These suggestions and recommendations are by no means the final word on what can, or should, be done to assist the victims of stalking. We believe, though, that they provide a basis to build upon, and that more can be done for the victims of stalking in particular and the victims of crime more generally.

Seek police assistance

This is absolutely essential and is the first course of action that should be taken. Since 1990, there has been a rapid adoption of anti-stalking laws across the US, Canada, Australia, the United Kingdom and New Zealand. Similar laws have been enacted in Europe. These laws have been enacted to assist and protect victims. But laws are only effective if the victims seek assistance. Stalking needs to be reported to the police so they may assist in preventing the stalker from committing more heinous crimes such as assault, sexual assault, or murder. Sometimes, if stalking occurs without violence or threatened violence, the police may not take the complaint seriously. If this occurs, contact a supervisor or the relevant prosecuting authority to press the issue.

Document all instances of stalking

Victims are not trained witnesses and do not know what information to volunteer to the police. It is important to help the police to build a case against the stalker. Victims should document all instances of stalking by making contemporaneous notes of any incident, however minor it may seem; keep copies of all threatening letters and other items sent by the stalker such as emails, phone messages, telephone records and gifts; be mindful of possible fingerprints and DNA when handling all items received; and take photos of injuries, property damage or of the stalker sitting outside your home or following you. Perishable items such as flowers and food items should be photographed and any delivery cards or other paperwork kept. Graffiti should also be photographed, with a particular emphasis on wording or symbols. Remember, Lester Worthington used to draw a smiley face, which he left as a pathetic and macabre form of calling card.

Develop a safety plan

Developing a safety plan is of the utmost importance. Simply put, the police cannot provide protection twenty-four hours a day, seven days a week. It is a sad and unfortunate reality that, if you are a victim of stalking, you are going to have to consider making changes to your lifestyle. You are going to have to assume responsibility for your own safety.

Don't be ashamed or reluctant to tell friends, neighbors and co-workers of your plight. Not only is it important for your own safety but for theirs as well. At the workplace, consider displaying a photo of the stalker and work with managerial, security and human resources staff to increase safety and security. At home, consider the installation of a security system and identifying a safe place to go to if you have to leave quickly.

Program your mobile phone with the contact numbers for police and victims assistance agencies. Victim assistance agencies can be an excellent source of support and can provide information about safety planning. If telephone harassment is a component of the stalking obtain an unlisted phone number. Where practical, vary the time and route you take to work and other places and try and travel with others present.

Consider applying for a Restraining Order

While there is some debate among academics about the merits of taking out a restraining order in stalking cases, it is an option that should be seriously considered. Restraining orders (also known as intervention, protection, or apprehended violence orders) can place specific restrictions on the stalker's contact with the victim that can include communications, approaches, or other forms of harassment. Breaches of the order can result in harsh sanctions, including imprisonment. Violating a restraining order allows the police to intervene on your behalf and the stalker can be arrested and charged by the police with a criminal offence. Where possible, consider using the following recording equipment to safely gather admissible evidence to be used in the application of a restraining order: audio recorder, video recorder, digital recorder or CCTV footage.

Threat Management Unit

We recommend that police services follow the lead of the Los Angeles Police Department (LAPD) and establish a designated Threat Management Unit to investigate stalking cases. The LAPD Threat Management Unit was established in 1990 and investigates serious threat cases within the City of Los Angeles. These include:

- aggravated stalking and criminal threats
- threats to elected public officials, and
- workplace violence involving Los Angeles city employees.

The most significant responsibility of the Threat Management Unit is undertaking a threat assessment, and developing a case management strategy. According to Detective Dunn of the LAPD Threat Management Unit, the threat assessment process is a 'multifaceted approach to evaluating the person(s) responsible for the threat being investigated. It involves the evaluation of the threat itself, the content and the context in which it was made.' Also, an evaluation is made regarding the vulnerability of the victim and in-depth research is conducted on the suspect, the suspect's behaviors and actions. Dunn observes that threats become more serious when they progress from less personal modes of contact to more personal modes; and that, when this occurs, it is time for the police to consider intervention options and 'slow the building momentum'.

Evidential provisions to assist victims

We firmly believe that evidentiary provisions must be tilted in favor of victims. Several states in the US have adopted a variety of evidentiary rules in stalking cases, which tilt the balance in favor of victims. For instance, in Oklahoma, repeated contact after the victim requests no further contact creates 'a rebuttable presumption that the victim felt terrorized, frightened, intimidated, threatened harassed or molested.' There is also an extensive list of the activities that constitute 'unconsented contact'. Washington State has legislated that there is prima facie evidence that the defendant intends to frighten, intimidate, or harass if the defendant continues to have contact with the victim after notice that the victim does not want contact.

Notification of Prisoner Status and Parole Hearings

Notifying a victim when the stalker is to be released from custody is an extremely important right for victims. It ensures that the criminal justice system remains engaged with victims. Washington State has one of the most detailed notification programs, which requires that notice must be given to the victim, chief of police, sheriff and school board. The law requires that a victim be notified if the victim makes a request for notification. In California, a victim can request through the Board of

Parole Hearings to appear before the hearing panel and make a statement.

Compensation and Restitution

All victims of stalking should have a statutory right to restitution or compensation. Restitution should be ordered in every case that a stalker is convicted regardless of the sentence or disposition. If the stalker is not in a position to pay then a state crime victim's tribunal should award compensation. In this way victims can be compensated for pain and suffering, lost earnings, damaged property, transportation expenses to court and non-reimbursed costs for counseling.

A NOTE ON SOURCES

In writing this book we have drawn on a range of sources. This has included publicly available court records, academic references and the Internet. We consulted with Joan and every member of her family, Detective Howard Bradley and Detective Wood, Attorneys at Law, Chuck Nachand and Marian Birge, members of the San Diego District Attorney's office and various witnesses who wished to remain un-named.

At the request of Joan and the authorities, we did not speak to Lester or any member of his family. The court records speak for themselves.

The following is a list of the references used in this book and in particular Part III: Stalking Resources:

Bran Nicol, *Stalking*, New York: Reakation Books Ltd., 2006.

Brown v. Plata et al: 563U.S. (2011).

Criminal Harassment (stalking) Canada: http://www.statcan.gc.ca/pub/85-005-x/2011001/article/11407-eng.htm.

Consultation on Stalking (UK): https://www.gov.uk/government/uploads/system/uploads/attachment_data/file/157898/consultation.pdf.

David J. Kapley and John R. Cooke, 'Trends in Ant stalking Legislation', in Debra A. Pinals (Ed.) *Stalking: Psychiatric Perspectives and Practical Approaches*. New York: Oxford University Press, 2007.

Department of Justice, 'Attorney General Eric Holder leads Stalking Awareness Event,' http://www.justice.gov/opa/pr/2011/January/11-ag-059.html, accessed 10 April 2012.

Department of Justice Canada: http://www.justice.gc.ca/eng/rp-pr/cj-jp/fv-vf/har/part1.html.

Diagnostic and Statistical Manual of Mental Disorders, Fourth Edition (DSM-IV), 1994.

Diana Lamplugh, 'Foreword' in Paul Infield and Graham Platford, *The Law of Harassment of Stalking*. London: Butterworth's, 2000.

Eigner v. Worthington (1997) http://law.justia.com/cases/california/court-of-appeal/4th/57/188.html.

Emma Ogilvie, Stalking: Legislative, Policing and Prosecution Patterns in Australia. Australian Institute of Criminology, Research and Public Policy Series No. 34, 2000.

Heather Mac Donald, *California's Prison-Litigation Nightmare: Activist judges are forcing the state to release prisoners—and crime is spiking*, City Journal, Autumn 2013, http://www.city-journal.org/2013/23_4_california-prisons.html.

Jeff Dunn, 'Operations of the LAPD Threat Management Unit' in J Reid Meloy, Lorraine Sheridan, Jens Hoffman (Eds.), Stalking, Threatening, and Attacking Public Figures. New York: Oxford University Press, 2008.

Joel Best, *Random Violence: How We Talk about New Crimes and New Victims*. Berkley and Los Angeles: University of California Press: 1999.

Keith E. Davis PhD, Irene Hanson Frieze PhD, and Roland D. Maiuro (Eds.), *Stalking: Perspectives on Victims and Perpetrators*. New York, NY: Springer Publishing, Inc., 2002.

Keith E. Davis, Irene Hanson Frieze, and Roland D. Maiuro (Eds.), 'Preface', *Stalking: Perspectives on Victims and Perpetrators*. Broadway: Springer Publishing Company, Inc., 2002.

J. Reid Meloy (Ed), *The Psychology of Stalking: Clinical and Forensic Perspectives*, San Diego, Academic Press, 1998.

J. Reid Meloy, Loraine Sheridan and Jens Hoffman (Eds), *Stalking, Threatening and Attacking Public Figures: A Psychological and Behavioural Analysis*, New York, Oxford University Press, 2008.

Mary P. Brewster (Ed), *Stalking: Psychology, Risk Factors, Interventions and Law*, New Jersey, Civic Research Institute, 2003.

Melita Schaum and Karen Parrish, Stalked: Breaking the Silence on the Crime of Stalking in America. New York: Pocket Books, 1995.

Michelle Pathe, *Surviving Stalking*, Cambridge University Press, 2002.

National Centre for Victims of Crime: Stalking Fact Sheet: National Centre for Victims of Crime; Stalking Fact Sheet: http://www.victimsofcrime.org/docs/src/stalking-fact-sheet_english.pdf?sfvrsn=4.

National Institute of Justice

http://www.nij.gov/topics/crime/stalking/pages/welcome.aspx

Network for surviving stalking: http://www.nss.org.uk

Office of Victim and Survivor Rights and Services@ http://www.cdcr.ca.gov/Victim_Services/Victim_Rights.html, accessed on 28 September 2012.

Paul Bocij, *Cyberstalking: Harassment in the Internet age and how to protect your family*, Westport: Praeger Publishers, 2008.

Paul E. Mullen, Michele Pathe, Rosemary Purcell, *Stalkers and Their Victims*. Cambridge: Cambridge University Press, 2000.

Robert J. Meadows, *Understanding Violence and Victimization*. New Jersey: Pearson Prentice Hall, 2013.

Samuel C. McQuade, Sarah E. Gentry, Nathan W. Fisk, Marcus K. Roger, *Cyberstalking and Cyberbullying*, New York, NY: Chelsea House, an Infobase Learning Company, 2012.

Stalking Awareness Month January 2014: http://stalkingawarenessmonth.org/about.

Stalking on the rise in Canada: http://news.nationalpost.com/2011/03/03/stalking-on-rise-in-canada-statscan/.

'Stalking Risk Profile', https://www.stalkingriskprofile.com/victim-support/restraining-orders, accessed 6 October 2012.

Three Judge Panel and California Inmate Population Reduction, Fact Sheet, California Department of Corrections and Rehabilitation, 23 May 2011.

Timeline: The Three Judge Court and California Inmate Population Reduction, Fact Sheet, California Department of Corrections and Rehabilitation, 19 November 2013.

US Bureau of Justice Statistics, http://www.bjs.gov/index.cfm?ty=tp&tid=973.

'What is stalking', http://www.police.nsw.gov.au/community_issues/domestic__and__family_violence/what_is_stalking.

Wikipedia.

About the Authors

Jackie Eigner is the daughter of Joan Eigner. She holds a Masters Degree in Criminology and a Bachelors Degree in Sociology. She is a Manager of strategic intelligence and has worked in Australian law enforcement for nearly thirteen years. She lives in Australia with her family.

Simon Gullifer is a highly experienced criminal investigator and has worked in Australian law enforcement for twenty-six years. He is a recipient of the National Medal for Service and a range of law enforcement accolades. He holds a Masters Degree in Diplomacy and Trade and a Bachelors Degree in Economics He is an avid reader and devotee of American history.

www.ingramcontent.com/pod-product-compliance
Lightning Source LLC
Chambersburg PA
CBHW052129270326
41930CB00012B/2812